INN AND AROUND LONDON

A HISTORY OF YOUNG'S PUBS

BY HELEN OSBORN

YOUNG & CO'S BREWERY PLC · WANDSWORTH · LONDON SW18 4JD

INN AND AROUND LONDON

A HISTORY OF YOUNG'S PUBS

BY HELEN OSBORN

CONTENTS

Published by Young & Co's Brewery PLC
The Ram Brewery · Wandsworth
London SW18 4JD
Telephone 081-870 0141

Edited, designed and typeset by Hardman Press Services
PO Box 30 · London SW19 5DT
Telephone 081-944 7955

Printed by Surrey Fine Art Press Ltd, Richmond-upon-Thames

ISBN 0 9518167 0 5

Introduction

It is hard to imagine England without its pubs. Whether they have witnessed dramatic historical events or merely existed in a backwater, pubs have always been central to the life of a community: as a convivial meeting place, a place for sports and games, for meals, or a stopping point on a journey. All the pubs in this book are run by Youngs, the South London independent brewers, and many of them have been Young's houses since the Young family first started brewing in Wandsworth in 1831. Such continuity is remarkable over two centuries that have otherwise seen enormous changes.

Some of the pubs described here have ancient origins, as far back as the Middle Ages, more were large coaching inns, built to serve the growing coaching trade in the 17th and 18th centuries, and many are the product of Victorian speculative building in South London when the railways brought so much development in their wake. In the mid-Victorian period, it was not uncommon for the pubs to be built before the houses in a street, their first customers being hundreds of thirsty building workers.

While researching material for this book I became aware of how much and how rapidly London expanded in the 19th century. Many of the places that now seem totally part of London were only villages or hamlets when Youngs first started supplying beer in 1831. Battersea, Clapham, Tooting, Hammersmith, Fulham, the list goes on and on.

Since the public house is so much a part of the character of an area, I have divided the book into geographical locations rather than listing the houses in alphabetical order — except in the case of the former H.H. Finch pubs, which were acquired by Young & Co in August 1991. These are dealt with separately in the chapter beginning on Page 138. I hope this proves easy to follow.

The Ram Brewery yard in the 1920s.

Charles Allen Young (left), the Brewery House in Wandsworth High Street, and John Allen Young.

The Young family and brewing in Wandsworth

The River Wandle, once the most worked river in England, has seen a great many industries come and go along its journey from Croydon and Carshalton to the Thames: hat making, fulling, dyeing, tanning, flour milling and, of course, brewing. In 1831, when Youngs first became involved in brewing at Wandsworth, there were 90 mills along the Wandle. While all these other trades have waxed and waned the Ram Brewery, near the river's mouth, has been on the same site, gently expanding over the years since 1675. This date is taken to be the start of the Ram Brewery's history since it is when first written mention of it occurs, but it is likely to be older still.

In 1675, the brewery was owned by a family called Draper, who had family connections with Jacob Tonson, secretary of the famous Kit Kat club, and it was for the Drapers that the Brewery House, facing Wandsworth High Street, was probably built. This house, now brewery offices, is early 18th century and has two fine plaster casts of Inigo Jones and Andrea Palladio in one of the front rooms. The Drapers, with their links through Jacob Tonson, seemed to have moved in the sort of social circles where such famous architectural names would have been well known. These plaster casts are thought to be the work of Italian craftsmen working in London. In 1763, however, the Drapers sold the brewery, the house and the Ram Inn (renamed the Brewery Tap in 1974) to Thomas Tritton. The Tritton family owned the brewery for another 68 years, expanding it to the east. (It was not until many years later, after the Young family took over, that the brewery site grew to adjoin the River Wandle on the west, York Road — now Ram Street — on the east, and what is now Armoury Way to the north.)

In 1803, the Surrey Iron Railway was opened. It was the first public railway independent of a canal to be sanctioned by Parliament and was paid for by subscription from local industrialists, among them Florance Young, a local benefactor, magistrate and High Sheriff of Surrey. Horses pulled the wagons along the iron track, which ran from just north of the Ram Brewery, near the Thames, through Earlsfield, Colliers Wood and Mitcham to Croydon. Some of the stone sleepers are still to be seen in the brewery wall. Unfortunately, the line was soon superseded by the invention of the steam locomotive and was closed in 1846.

The Surrey Iron Railway: detail from an early 19th-century painting that hangs in the brewery boardroom.

When Thomas Tritton died in 1786, he left the business to his son George and when George died, the brewery came into the hands of the Young family when George's widow sold it to Charles Allen Young, son of Florance Young, and his partner Anthony Fothergill Bainbridge on 23 November 1831. The purchase price seems to have been in the region of £140,000, with the site around half its present size.

Charles Allen Young was 44, married with seven children and with established connections in the brewing industry through his back-making business. (Backs are shallow vats used both in brewing and dyeing.) Only five months after the purchase, on 13 March 1832, the brewery suffered a severe fire and the building housing the copper was entirely destroyed. The fire was thought to be arson and according to a report in John Bull, the parish fire engine had its hoses cut, making it useless, and the work of

Extract from John Bull, 19 March 1832, reporting a fire at the Ram Brewery

DESTRUCTION OF MESSRS. TRITTON'S BREWERY BY FIRE.—About a quarter before five o'clock on Tuesday morning the brewery at Wandsworth, Surrey, known till lately as Tritton's, was discovered to be on fire ; and before it was possible to extinguish the flames the whole of that part of the building designated the copper-house was entirely destroyed. The exterior of the copper is now exposed to the gaze of the traveller, and the whole range of that portion of the premises is reduced to a heap of ruins. The present proprietors, Messrs. Young and Bainbridge, have, we understand, but recently become possessed of the establishment, for which we have heard they gave a sum approaching very nearly in amount to 140,000l. It is said that the fire, which originated in the steam-engine department of the brewery, is suspected to be the work of some evil-disposed persons, for the purpose of plunder. When the parish fire-engine arrived at the premises it was rendered totally useless, through some villains having cut the hose. On the arrival of the firemen of the Phœnix, Assurance, and other offices, their efforts were much impeded by a set of low fellows, who fell to drinking the porter on the premises.— The property is said to be insured in the Imperial Assurance Com-

the firemen was "much impeded by a set of low fellows, who fell to drinking the porter on the premises". This setback was soon overcome, however, and in 1835, Young & Bainbridge installed the first of two beam engines, which are still in working order today. They had already taken over leases on many of the local public houses from the Tritton family and 1836 saw the first purchase of a freehold outright. The majority of beer being brewed at this time would probably have been porter.

Charles Allen Young died in 1855 and his son Charles Florance Young, aged 33, became partner to Anthony Bainbridge. These mid-Victorian years were ones of consolidation and gentle expansion — more pubs were bought and leased, and production rose. In 1867, the second beam engine was installed. Later, the second generation of Bainbridges entered the partnership, Herbert Bainbridge. In 1882, a second disastrous fire occurred in the tun room block, but this was rebuilt the following year.

The next 20 years were to see enormous changes. In 1884, the partnership with Bainbridge was dissolved and Charles Florance Young, then 62 and a grandfather, carried on with other family members as Young & Co. When Charles Florance died in 1890, the decision was taken to issue shares and become a limited company. The new company was incorporated on 17 November 1890 with seven shareholders. The late 1880s and the 1890s saw a rush of public houses bought as leases came up for renewal. There was a huge amount of speculation on pubs in London in these years as all the brewers sought to consolidate their estates. The new company probably needed every penny it could raise from its shareholders to meet these demands.

Production continued to rise and by the end of the century, the brewery site was much as it is today. A canal, known as the Cut, had been built from the Thames to the brewery for barges to deliver coal and other supplies. In 1922, this was the cause of a flood that unfortunately destroyed many early records. The Cut was finally filled in in 1935. The brewery chimney was built in 1903 to replace four earlier chimneys. Trade in bottled beer began in 1905.

The first half of the 20th century saw a more gradual expansion in pubs and trade. The Second World War meant that once again the brewery saw damage and fire with the destruction of the cask shed and major damage to the Brewery Tap. In 1955, the A ordinary shares were floated on the Stock Exchange. In 1961, Foster-Probyn Ltd, a long-established bottling concern, was bought. The business was moved to the Ram Brewery from Islington in 1972.

The present chairman, John Allen Young, great-great-grandson of Charles Allen Young, joined the company in 1954.

In 1973, the wine shippers and merchants, Cockburn & Campbell, were acquired and in 1984, with demand outstripping capacity, a new brewhouse was completed and some equipment that had been in use for more than 100 years .was replaced. The beam engines now are used only for demonstration purposes, but are kept in good working order.

The Cut in 1930, with the brewery in the background.

In 1991, Young & Co bought the long-established family firm, H.H. Finch Ltd, and its chain of London pubs, an acquisition that is dealt with in some detail in the chapter beginning on Page 138.

The number of shareholders in Young & Co has now risen to just over 5,000, but it is still a family business, with many employees also serving generation after generation.

Balham

Balham High Road, like Tooting High Street, was once part of Stane Street, the Roman road from Chichester to London. Balham is the Saxon for home of Bealga, an isolated homestead rather than a village. The manors of Balham are linked with those of Streatham and Tooting and it does not appear to have had a distinctive, separate existence until the 18th century.

An 1827 lease of the **Duke of Devonshire** was first assigned to Young & Bainbridge in 1832 and the pub was bought in 1925. Although now large and imposing, in the style of a gin palace, it was originally a beer house, without a spirit licence. It was doing a brisk trade, however, and an 1857 entry in the Young & Bainbridge property book

Duke of Devonshire
39 Balham High Road
London SW12
081-673 1363
*A large pub with
magnificent wood and
glasswork.*
Discus skittles.
Tables outside.
Function room.

remarks: "This is a very valuable House. It does a large and increasing trade. Till last year it was unable to obtain a spirit licence. It is let to the present Tenant at £60 per annum but it is well worth £120. The trade has been 613 (butts) Porter but so large a quantity is not likely to be consumed should other houses be opened." Whether this remark means that the Duke of Devonshire was the only pub at this time in the area, or whether it was just the only Young's house is left unsaid. The discus skittle alley from the Duke's Head, Putney, (see Page 88) has been moved here. Discus skittles claims to be the forerunner of all later forms of skittles and is reputed to have started in Norwich in the 15th century. Once, many large and medium-sized pubs had skittle alleys, but now they are very rare.

Grove
39 Oldridge Road
London SW12
081-673 6531
*Large unspoilt old pub
with beautiful decorated
ceiling in the saloon bar.*

The land for the **Grove** was bought by Young & Bainbridge in 1870 and the pub was built between 1873 and 1877. For some time before this (since at least 1857), Young & Bainbridge had been renting the land with a house known as Holly Grove. Oldridge Road had not been built. Thus the name of the Grove is a reminder of the

The Grove in 1922, before the building was extended into Bellamy Street on the right.

Nightingale
97 Nightingale Lane
London SW12
081-673 1637
Small, friendly local.
Garden. Tables at front.

house that preceded it. Since being built, the Grove has altered very little in appearance and inside retains the original fine plaster work.

The **Nightingale** was bought by Young & Co in 1920. It was built as a pub (although differing greatly in style from the Grove and the Duke of Devonshire) on the Old Park Estate, which was divided up into lots and sold for the building of detached and semi-detached villas in 1869. The owners of the estate were obviously anxious to avoid allowing anyone but the wealthy middle class to live there as no house could be built to be sold for less than £800 — a large amount of money in 1869 — and no house was allowed within 25 feet of the road. It is hard to say whether Nightingale Lane (formerly Balham Wood Lane) has been named after the pub or whether the pub has been named after the lane. Some authorities say the area was known for the song of nightingales and the use of "lane" testifies to the rural origin of this part of Balham.

The Nightingale just after the First World War. The pub is virtually unchanged outside today (below).

Barking

Barking was an early Anglo-Saxon settlement and Barking Abbey was founded in 666. At the beginning of the 19th century, Barking was much larger than the surrounding villages, with a population of 8,000 by 1831. It had attracted the wealthy gentry since the 18th century and the most important industry was fishing. In 1833, there were 140 vessels and the fleet was famous.

Britannia
1 Church Road
Barking
Essex
081-594 1305
Large, comfortable pub.

The **Britannia** pub carries a reminder of the seafaring days of Barking with caryatids around the outside of the pub being reminiscent of a ship's prow. With the growth of the railways, the fishing trade declined as it became more economical to send fish by rail from the North East coast rather than by boat up the Thames to London. In 1899, the town ceased to be a port altogether, but already factory sites were beginning to grow up.

The Britannia was built between 1848 and 1863 on the Dove-House Estate, which was sold for building in 1850. Church Road, only a footpath in 1800, was probably the first road on the estate. The Britannia is described in A History of Barking by J. Frogley (written in 1900): "The old house was a square, bricked, double fronted and entered by three steps, with bay windows on each side. On the left of the doorway was the bar and on the right the tap room. In 1868 the tenant was a Mr Lewis and he was succeeded by Mr Alister of Creeksmouth, and during his time the house was nearly re-built, but not larger. He died there in 1881, and the same year the Freehold was sold by auction." In 1887, it was sold again to the Kitson family, who owned it until 1965 when it was sold to Youngs. It was again redesigned, this time for the Kitsons in 1898 by the famous Victorian architect Frederick W. Ashton. The busty caryatids on the outside walls were one of the hallmarks of Ashton's East London pubs and examples survive elsewhere.

Ashton's caryatids adorning the exterior of the Britannia.

*The White Hart
in Victorian days
(right) and in the
1920s (far right).*

Barnes

Barnes takes its name from the Anglo-Saxon word for a barn. A small village on the banks of the Thames, it was originally part of the manor of Mortlake, and Rocque's map of 1721-9 shows Mortlake as the bigger place. The manor house at Barn Elms was for many years a more important place than Barnes itself. Walsingham, Secretary of State to Elizabeth I, rented the house, entertained the Queen and held councils there.

White Hart
The Terrace
Riverside
London SW13
081-876 5177
*Splendid old pub backing
on to the Thames near the
end of the Boat Race
course.*
Riverside terrace.
Function room.

The three Young's pubs in Barnes were originally three of only four pubs in all the village and so must have had great influence within the community. The **White Hart** is perhaps the oldest, dating back to 1662, and The Terrace is part of the older Tudor layout of the roads in Barnes. The earliest written reference to the White Hart is in 1676, when it was called the King's Arms, and is a transfer from Robert Warner, cooper, on his death to his son, Charles. The Warner family held the pub until 1736. The Bucknalls then had it until 1766 when it came into the Trevy family of Putney and around this time first became known as the

*The White Hart during
the 1990 Boat Race.*

White Hart. Young & Bainbridge bought it in 1857. From 1863 to 1878, it was used for Masonic meetings by the Rose of Denmark Lodge. It was extensively rebuilt at the turn of the century, giving it a grand Edwardian air and adding balconies for the crowds watching the Boat Race. For some time, it was used as a hotel. Unfortunately, it has lost the stone inscribed 1662, which used to be over the entrance.

Bull's Head
373 Lonsdale Road
London SW13
081-876 5241
A grand building with comfortable bars. World famous for its jazz music. Stables Restaurant approached from High Street.

The **Bull's Head** was originally called the King's Head and is first mentioned in 1672, but it had become the Bull's Head by 1748. It was assigned to Young & Bainbridge in 1831 from an 1820 lease. It was rebuilt by the freeholder in 1845 and at that time was next to a busy wharf, which must have provided much trade for the pub, though it appears this custom was seasonal. The Young & Bainbridge property valuation of 1857 notes that the Bull's Head "tho' large and commodious hardly affords a living in the winter scarcely doing any business." The pub was altered in 1874 and Youngs bought it in 1896. After the wharf trade ended, the Bull's Head was a large and expensive pub to run and went into something of a decline but since the 1960s, it has enjoyed a renaissance as a renowned jazz pub. World

Jazz at the Bull's Head in the 1990s and (right) the pub in the 1920s.

famous musicians now play there and it is as important a venue as Ronnie Scott's, with radio broadcasts and recordings being made from the music room at the back.

The **Coach and Horses**, just round the corner from the Bull's Head, was first leased by Young & Bainbridge in 1831 and is much the smallest of the three pubs in Barnes. The earliest it can definitely be traced to is 1818, when it was run by Philip Butler. The High Street is also one of the oldest roads in Barnes and away from the influences of the river trade, the Coach and Horses has retained a more villagey character than the grander Victorian and Edwardian expansions of the Bull's Head and White Hart.

Coach and Horses
27 High Street
London SW13
081-878 2538
Small, busy and full of character.
Garden.

The Coach and Horses in the 1920s.

Battersea

Battersea is another ancient village, its name meaning marshy island and known once for its market gardens, particularly for asparagus, which is said to have been brought to Battersea from France by the Huguenots. The **Castle**, although now a modern building, was originally built around 1600. This part of Battersea, near the river, is the oldest. Apart from the market gardens that covered the area around Battersea Bridge and Lavender Hill, most of the rest of the parish was marshland.

Castle
115 Battersea High Street
London SW11
071-228 8181
A modern building with two bars.
Garden.
Conservatory.

The original carved sign of the Castle, said by some to be Elizabethan and a very fine example of the kind, has been preserved on the side of the new building. Carved signs of this type are now increasingly rare. The sign was rediscovered in 1950 during redecoration under many layers of paint. The Castle became a coaching inn and had a first-floor bay window into which passengers could tread straight from the tops of coaches. It was one of a number of inns mentioned in 1789 in Companion from London to Brighthelmston by J. Edwards. The pub was first leased by

The carved wooden sign on the old Castle and (above right) the pub exterior after the First World War. Right: the new Castle on opening day in 1965, with the restored wooden sign on the gable end of the building.

Young & Bainbridge in 1843 and was bought in 1891. In the 1857 valuation of pubs, a comment in the Young & Bainbridge property book notes: "These premises are old and require somewhat heavy repairs from time to time. They are held for 17³₄ years at £28 and are let to a very indifferent and unenergetic tenant at £40 per annum. Considered to be worth £50 (per annum)". The old Castle was demolished as part of a council scheme for flats in 1963. During excavations for the modern building in 1964-65, workmen's shovels broke a buried pot containing 49 gold sovereigns, 34 half-sovereigns and some silver. All the coins were dated from 1829 to 1893. It was declared treasure trove but a sovereign and a half-sovereign were bought back by Youngs and set under the foundation stone for the new pub.

Duke of Cambridge
228 Battersea Bridge Road
London SW11
071-223 5662
*Street-corner local
transformed into an
imposing period pub with
two separate bars.*
Tables at front.

The **Duke of Cambridge** was built in the early 1860s and became a Young & Bainbridge house in 1864. The land around Battersea Bridge at the end of the 18th century had all been market gardens. But between 1825 and 1864, the population of Battersea rose from around 4,000 to around 54,000. This change from village to suburb was precipitated by the first wooden Battersea Bridge, built by Earl Spencer in 1776. The link with Chelsea inevitably began to bring development over the river and Battersea started to become fashionable. Daniel Lysons, writing in 1792, said of the bridge that it "now begins to have the effect of increasing the number of buildings, above 20 houses having lately been erected". The modern Battersea Bridge and Battersea Bridge Road were built in 1890.

The Duke of Cambridge's stables were once used by a volunteer fire brigade before the London Fire Brigade was founded. The Duke of Cambridge was also the terminus for one of the last horse-drawn omnibuses, the number 34 from Islington to Battersea. Omnibuses had originally come to Battersea in 1839, superseding the coach service, but were themselves quickly followed by the railway, at Nine Elms in 1838 and at Clapham Junction in 1846. As a continuation of the coaching trade, pubs were very often the termini for horse-drawn omnibuses in London since they already had stabling facilities. This may be why some London buses still terminate at public houses in an echo of coaching days.

*The Duke of Cambridge
in the early 1920s (left)
and after its 1989
refurbishment.*

In 1989, the Duke of Cambridge was extensively refurbished and restored, using original Victorian panels and decorated glass. As a result, it won the 1990 Design for Leisure Award.

Beddington

Roman buildings have been found at Beddington and the evidence suggests that it was possibly a Roman station. More recently, Beddington has been dominated by the large house and estate of Beddington Park, once owned by the Carew family. Apart from Beddington Park, the village was no more than a hamlet until the 20th century. In Greater London (1895), Walford says of Beddington: "The village . . . contains but scattered houses and can scarcely boast of a main street." Walford goes on to describe the **Plough** as a "little old fashioned inn".

The present building seems to be one in a series of pubs. The previous building was early 18th century, brick-built with four bays and shutters on the ground-floor windows, and had a series of barns or outhouses, which may have contained an even earlier pub. The earliest written mention seems to be in 1785 when the Licensed Victuallers' Records show Joseph Simpson as the landlord. For very many years, the Plough was the only inn in Beddington. The architect for the present building was J. Barker and it was built in 1897. Young & Co had taken up the new lease in 1896 and bought it in 1925.

At one time, caves on the opposite side of Plough Lane were used by the tenant as a cellar. Partly natural and partly

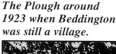

Plough
Croydon Road
Beddington
Surrey
081-647 1122
*A large, imposing pub
with two bars.*

*The Plough around
1923 when Beddington
was still a village.*

the result of sand excavation, they were rumoured in the 19th century to be the hiding place of robbers. They may have been used for rum-smuggling in the 18th and early 19th centuries and there are stories of trains of donkeys carrying smuggled goods being seen at night crossing the downs in the direction of Beddington. The Plough is said to be haunted by the ghost of a man in a cap and objects have been moved around by a mysterious presence.

Betchworth

Dolphin
The Street
Betchworth
Surrey
0737-842288
Classic village pub with three beamed bars, one with flagstone floor.
Garden.

The **Dolphin** is said to be more than 400 years old, although the building dates from the mid to late 18th century. It is listed as a building of architectural and historic interest. The earliest definite written mention is 1785 when the Licensed Victuallers' Records show Richard Staning as landlord. The Staning family were still there in 1825. Until recently, it was the property of the Betchworth House Estate, whose agent used to collect rent on quarter days in one of the inn's rooms. M. Ryan, in her book Betchworth Within Living Memory, mentions a large room that was used for dances and other village festivities before the Village Hall was built. This room may have been in an outbuilding for today the Dolphin has no large rooms. The Dolphin produced its own beer and cider until 1926 in a brewhouse to the left and back of the inn. In the yard there was a pump operated for brewing by a horse walking round and round in circles. The Dolphin also ran a carriage hire

The Dolphin in 1991.

service for local journeys. Nowadays, the outhouses, brewhouse, coach house and harness room have all gone and the area they occupied is part of the garden. The Dolphin still has its original stone floor and open log fires. The sign of the Dolphin is interesting because it belongs to the Watermen's Company and was also the sign of the Dauphin. The Dolphin was bought by Youngs in 1984.

Lamb
94 Lamb's Conduit Street
London WC1
071-405 0713
Splendid old pub with ornate glass and woodwork.
Paved garden at back.
Functions room.

Bloomsbury

The **Lamb** pub and Lamb's Conduit Street both owe their names to William Lamb, a gentleman of the Chapel Royal under Henry VIII and freebrother of the Clothworkers' Company. In 1577, he improved an existing conduit, originally built in 1498, to bring water down from the upper end of Red Lion Street, Holborn, through lead pipes to Snow Hill (about 2,000 yards) as an act of charity to benefit the neighbourhood. Lamb also gave "poor women" 120 pails to carry and serve the water in. The conduit was rebuilt in 1667 from a design by Sir Christopher Wren and was finally superseded in 1746 by a new conduit running near where the Lamb now stands.

The Lamb in 1956.

There were many springs and wells in the area and The Illustrated London News of 22 November 1851 records one man entering the pub yard "and with the assistance of mine host of the Lamb lifted the trapdoor on the pavement and descended by a short flight of steps into a brick vault. There with a stout cane for lack of a divining rod, he probed the soil until a hollow sound revealed at no great depth the wooden cover of the well". Because of reconstruction, this can no longer be done, but a plaque commemorates its existence.

This area of London was open fields until the 1720s. An old English herbal mentions cress and winter rocket growing "in the next pasture to the Conduit Head behind Gray's Inn". One old gentleman quoted in an 1857 edition of Notes and Queries spoke of the early 18th century when, after an attack of smallpox, he "was sent into the country to a row of houses standing on the west side of Lambs Conduit Street; that all the space before him was open fields; that a streamlet of water ran under his window; that he saw a man snipe shooting."

The Lamb was probably constructed in the first major

wave of building between 1720 and 1729 and is first recorded in 1729. Today, the building is a mixture of styles: some 18th-century parts remain but it was heavily "improved" in 1836 and 1876 and more recently in 1959, three years after it had become a Young's house. Charles Dickens may have visited the Lamb when he lived nearby in Doughty Street and the snob screens inside are an interesting remnant of the late Victorian era. These hinged, frosted-glass screens were a development of the 1890s, from the fixed counter screen, which had just enough room underneath for quart mugs of beer to be passed over the bar without the publican seeing who was being served. The hinged snob screen was considered to be an improvement because the bar staff could check on customers without disturbing their privacy. The Lamb had been a cider house until it was acquired by Youngs in 1956.

Calthorpe Street was built by the third Baron Calthorpe in two sections — the first from 1821 to 1826 and the

The Calthorpe Arms on the day it opened as a Young's pub in 1984.

Calthorpe Arms
252 Gray's Inn Road
London WC1
071-278 4732
A comfortable street-corner local.
Dining/functions room.
Tables outside.

second between 1842 and 1849. The **Calthorpe Arms** was once used as a temporary magistrates' court in the 19th century after the first recorded murder of a policeman on duty, Constable William Grantham of the Metropolitan Police. He was patrolling in Somers Town on the night of 29 June 1830 when he came across two drunken Irishmen fighting over a woman. He intervened, was knocked down and kicked to death by all three.

The numbers in Calthorpe Street were reassigned in 1876. Upper Calthorpe Street had been built as a residential street for gentry, while Lower Calthorpe Street contained small shops and was inhabited by traders and merchants. The Calthorpe Arms is listed in Victorian street directories as at 37 Gray's Inn Road, not at the present number 252. Youngs bought the Calthorpe Arms in 1984.

Bow

Coborn Arms
8 Coborn Road
London E3
081-980 3793
A comfortable and friendly local.
Tables at front.

The Coborn Arms, 1991.

The **Coborn Arms** and Coborn Road take their names from Mrs Priscilla Coborn, a wealthy benefactor to Bow. In her will of 1701, she left a fund for the benefit of seamen's widows with the income to come from her manor, Covill Hall, at White Roding in Essex. She also left an annuity to the clergy and the poor of Bow to be supported by income from her land north of the Bow Road. When this was covered in housing in the early to mid 19th century, the rents from the properties continued to benefit local people.

The earliest mention of the Coborn Arms is in the Home Counties Directory of 1845 (Bow was not then considered part of London). By 1853, it is listed in the London Directory, probably testimony to population rises in Bow.

Originally, the pub was only at number 8 Coborn Road. Number 10 was a barber's shop but is now part of the pub. The Coborn Arms was bought by Youngs in 1984 and was extended into the house on the other side (number 6) in 1985. The Coborn Arms and number 6 were both bought from the Coopers' Company and the Coborn Educational Trust, which had taken over from the Priscilla Coborn Foundation and still owns whole streets of property nearby.

Brixton

Both the Young's pubs in Brixton have 19th-century origins and are the result of London's southwards expansion. Brixton itself, although one of the ancient hundreds of Surrey, was not actually inhabited until the early 19th century, but existed only as a landmark — Brixi's stone.

Trinity Arms
45 Trinity Gardens
London SW9
071-274 4544
Two separate bars full of character.
Tables at front.

Right: the Trinity Arms in the 1920s.

Hope and Anchor
123 Acre Lane
London SW2
071-274 1787
Restored to its former glory as a traditional local.
Garden.

The **Trinity Arms** was built in 1850 and the square in which it stands was presumably laid out at the same time. Trinity Gardens is named after the Trinity Asylum in Acre Lane, which was founded in 1824 by Thomas Bailey for 12 poor women who professed belief in the Holy Trinity. When Young & Co took

over the pub in 1885, the lease included squatters' rights to the gardens opposite. These were not originally enclosed with railings, although they were by 1885. Youngs bought the Trinity Arms outright in 1911.

The **Hope and Anchor** is older and dates from at least 1815 when it is mentioned in the Licensed Victuallers' Records. In 1845, it was just the Hope but reverted to being the Hope and Anchor by 1853. It was rebuilt in 1889 with a bowling green. Young & Co bought the 1890 lease in 1891. When trade declined, it was decided to buy the freehold in 1933 and to rebuild a larger pub, which was opened in 1937. Games at the Hope and Anchor still include shove halfpenny and skittles.

The Hope and Anchor in the 1920s (left) and in 1940. Note that the tenant in the 1920s, W.F. Farmer, was also at the Trinity Arms.

CONTRACT.

We Messrs Young & Co Brewery Limited of Ram Brewery Wandsworth.

do hereby acknowledge myself to be the purchaser of the Property described in the within Particulars of Sale, for the sum of £ *16810. 0. 0* and that I have paid the sum of £ *1681* by way of deposit and in part payment of the purchase-money, to Messrs. HASLETT, as Auctioneers and Agents for the Vendor, *Alfred Louis Savage* and I hereby agree to pay the remainder of the said purchase-money, and the amount of the within-mentioned valuations and to complete the purchase according to the within Particulars and Conditions of Sale.

As witness my hand, this 17th day of July, 1922.

Purchase-money .... £ *16810. 0. 0*
Deposit .... £ *1681. 0. 0*
Balance payable, exclusive of Valuations, etc. £ *15129. 0. 0*

As Agents for the Vendor, *Alfred Louis Savage* we hereby ratify this Sale, and acknowledge the receipt of the said deposit of £ *1681. 0. 0*

Witness

Abstract of Title to be sent to *Messrs Pyke Franklin Gould 63 Lincoln Inn Fields WC*

The 1922 contract of sale for the Wickwood Tavern (left) and the pub at the time.

Camberwell

Coldharbour Lane is a mediaeval parish road connecting the settlements of Clapham, Brixton and Camberwell. By the 18th century, Camberwell was a village famous for flowers, fruit and butterflies: the Camberwell Beauty, once numerous in the fields here, took its name from the village. Development of the area began before 1830 but growth was slow at first and up to 1850, the land was still mainly pasture. Loughborough House had been owned by an eminent Royalist, Henry Hastings, who became Lord Loughborough in 1643. In 1854, however, it was pulled down for development and building work began to accelerate.

During the 1860s, the area was dissected by railway lines and the viaducts at Loughborough Junction, named after the old house, were completed in 1872, when the branch line to Peckham caused the demolition of houses in Flaxman Road only ten years after they had been built. The **Wickwood Tavern**, a large and typical mid-Victorian pub, was spared this fate. It had been built in 1868 on land from the Milkwood Estate. Youngs bought the pub in 1922 from the Savage family, who had held it for 43 years.

Wickwood Tavern
58 Flaxman Road
London SE5
071-274 5338
Victorian pub full of character and characters.
Functions room.

Camden Town
see Regent's Park (Page 90)

The Greyhound between the wars, showing its two distinct styles of architecture.

Carshalton

The ponds at Carshalton are the source for one arm of the Wandle and around them lies the oldest part of the village. Carshalton takes its name from the beds of cress that used to be grown here, probably to distinguish itself from the other Altons nearby.

Greyhound
2 High Street
Carshalton
Surrey
081-647 1511
Old pub with many rooms of differing style and character.
Hotel rooms.
Functions.

The earliest reference to the **Greyhound** is 1706 and the London Journal of 15 June 1723 announces "a Cock Match to be fought at the Grey-Hound in Case-Houghton on the 17th, 18th and 19th of this instant, June, between the Gentlemen of Putney and the Gentlemen of Croydon. They fight for a considerable sum of money. To begin at 12 o'clock each day. Also a plate of £10 value will be run for the 19th day on Banstead Downs by horses that never run for £5, and the winning horse to be thrown dice for at £15 by those that run their horses. The weight 10 stone; Three heats. They are shown and enter'd at the Grey-Hound in Case-Houghton the Monday before they run."

It seems that the Greyhound was at the centre of a considerable sporting initiative in this part of Surrey as its sign indicates, although it may also be connected with the arms of the Gaynesford family, who owned Stone Court at Carshalton. It was surrounded by good hunting country and there would also have been coursing and cock fighting. The Greyhound is mentioned in many 18th-century advertisements for meets and matches.

When first built, it was the only inn on the Gaynesford Estate and the oldest part of the building is the beer cellar and kitchens. In an 1829 lease it is described as "all that old messuage or tenement with the brewhouse, millhouse, lower stables, yard, outhouses, buildings . . .", obviously a large and sprawling establishment.

The pub was leased by Henry Young in 1834 and sublet to Young & Bainbridge from 1846. It was at this time that the brick and stone portion of the pub was built or rebuilt (1837-40). The Young & Bainbridge property book entry reads "The House has been greatly improved by us and does a fair business." Henry's son William Allen Young became the leaseholder in 1860 (when it still included a brewhouse) and it was finally transferred to the company in 1861.

For many years, horses kept at the Greyhound were used to help pull carts out of the mud of the ponds when they got stuck. Until after the Second World War, the Greyhound was an hotel and is said to be haunted by the ghost of a cloaked traveller who was found frozen on the doorstep one winter's night. In 1969, while renovations were being carried out, a mosaic of a greyhound was found, which was thought to be the work of Italian craftsmen 200 years ago. The Greyhound is a listed building.

Catford

The village of Catford dates from the 13th century. Until the urban sprawl of London reached here in the late 19th century, Catford was an outlying hamlet of the village of Lewisham, as were Hither Green and Rushey Green. Lewisham High Street was the only road through the village and was once lined with elm trees.

Catford Ram
9 Winslade Way
London SE6
081-690 6206
Modern pub in traditional style.

The **Catford Ram** is a new building, opened in 1974, opposite Lewisham Town Hall and part of the new Catford Town Centre. The land was originally part of the Springfield Park Estate, which appears to have been broken up for building plots in 1882. This is the only Young's pub and one of the few pubs in London to have its cellar above the pub instead of below. The beer has to be issued through special gravity-controlled pumps to the bar below to prevent flooding every time a pint is pulled. The Catford Ram is also unusual in having no windows, apart from those at the entrance doors.

Inside the Catford Ram, 1991.

Chelsea

Coopers' Arms
87 Flood Street
London SW3
071-376 3120
Victorian street-corner local with an international flavour.
Function room.

Chelsea Ram
Burnaby Street
London SW10
071-351 4008
Grand street-corner local.

The old village of Chelsea was originally situated around the Old Church (St Luke's) on the banks of the Thames. Flood Street was one of the village streets, first called Robinson's Row and then Queen Street. It was renamed Flood Street in the 1870s after Luke Thomas Flood, a resident of Cheyne Walk, who left £3,000 to Chelsea Parish on his death in 1860. The **Coopers' Arms** is shown as standing at 33 Queen Street in the 1846 Post Office Directory of London but any earlier history remains obscure. When Youngs took over the pub in 1990, Tom Wood, who works at the brewery as the last remaining cooper in London, went along to demonstrate his ancient craft skills from the back of a horse-drawn dray.

The **Chelsea Ram** is a product of the Victorian and Edwardian development of Chelsea. Burnaby Street and the

The Chelsea Ram in 1983, before it became a pub, and (far right) in 1991.

Lots Road area were laid out in the 1860s and 70s. The Chelsea Ram has had an odd history: although originally built as a pub, it had never succeeded in gaining a licence until Youngs, having bought the building in 1984, were granted a licence. Until then it had been used as a laundry depository, soup kitchen, bric à brac shop and garage repair shop. The Chelsea Ram is now visited by some of the pop and rock musicians who use a recording studio nearby.

Chertsey

Crown
London Street
Chertsey
Surrey
09325-64657
Large, impressive hotel in town centre, with many varied bars.
Hotel rooms.
Restaurant.
Function room.

The **Crown** was originally a coaching inn and is listed in the 1832 Pigot's Directory as supplying coaches to London. In 1822, it was being run by Thomas Thackham and as his name is also shown in the 1790 Licensed Victuallers' Records, we may assume that he was also at the Crown then. Chertsey attracted much coaching trade as there are a further 19 or 20 licensed premises also listed for the years 1785 to 1827. In the 1845 Home Counties Directory, it is listed as the Crown Hotel Commercial Inn. Chertsey was by then a small town with a population of 5,347.

The Crown was rebuilt at the end of the 19th century specifically for the hotel trade and became a Young's house in 1898. It was altered in 1937. By the 1950s, demand for hotels had steeply declined and it was decided to develop the Crown as a restaurant. Planning permission was granted in 1990 to restore the Crown to an hotel with the addition of 30 bedrooms.

The Crown, 1920.

Chislehurst

Chislehurst, whose name is derived from the Anglo-Saxon words for pebble and wood, has had some famous residents: Walsingham had a house here and Napoleon III came to Chislehurst after 1871 when he was exiled from France. He may perhaps have visited the **Bull's Head** as it has existed since at least 1753. The Kent Registry of Victuallers Recognizances is complete back to this date and the licensee of the Bull's Head was then Jacob Mann. As Jacob Mann is also listed as holding a licence in Chislehurst in 1743 it is probable that he was also at the Bull's Head at that date. In the 1845 Home Counties Directory, it is listed as one of six inns and taverns in Chislehurst.

The Bull's Head has had an unchanging role over the

Bull's Head
Royal Parade
Chislehurst
Kent
081-467 1727
Imposing old pub for all tastes.
Hotel rooms. Functions.
Restaurant.
Garden.

The Bull's Head, probably pictured in the 1940s.

years. Used as a coaching inn, with bedrooms, it evolved into a small hotel. Young & Co bought the Bull's Head, then known as the Bull Hotel, in 1931, but had been leasing it for some time before. It was damaged by bombs in 1945 but was quickly reopened. In the 1960s, the boxer Henry Cooper stayed at the Bull's Head while training for several of his championship fights and in 1969, the brewery chairman, John Young, presented Henry with a silver Shire horseshoe as a good luck charm. The Bull's Head has gained a reputation in recent years for its restaurant and plans have been drawn up for an extension to be built as an hotel.

Chiswick

Crown and Anchor
374 Chiswick High Road
London W4
081-995 2607
Spacious, street-corner local.
Function room.

The **Crown and Anchor** stands opposite Turnham Green, the site of a famous battle in 1642 between the Cavaliers and the Roundheads. Unfortunately, it seems unlikely that there was any pub there to witness the event as Turnham Green was described by one observer as a "plain".

King Charles had captured Brentford and, fearing for London, the Roundheads had arrived at Turnham Green with 24,000 men. Charles took fright and retreated to Kingston and most of the Londoners returned home. But Prince Rupert, with his "desperate route of Cavaliers", advanced on those still camped on Turnham Green. Hard and bloody fighting left Prince Rupert's men soundly beaten, with 800 dead. The Roundheads had 120 dead. After the Restoration, Turnham Green was a notorious place for highwaymen and footpads. The tone of the neighbourhood improved, however.

The Crown and Anchor appears to have been built in 1825 and was first leased by Young & Bainbridge in 1856. In 1831, Chiswick's total population was 4,994 and Turnham Green was described by Pigot's Middlesex Directory in 1839: "Very little business is carried on, but the houses are truly respectable and chiefly inhabited by persons who have residences for trade in London, or by those retired from business". The Crown and Anchor was one of 21 taverns. Few of the original houses along the High Road remain, although some 18th-century houses on the Green have survived.

In the Young & Bainbridge property book, the 1857 valuation entry reads "Held for 26 years at a peppercorn rent and let for £70. The next tenant to pay £80. It is a fair House of business and improved by the Barracks on the Green". Presumably this means that the trade was improved by the nearby presence of a barracks. The Crown and Anchor was bought by Young & Co in 1903 and extensively altered in 1936 with a new frontage.

The Crown and Anchor in the 1920s (left) and during the Second World War.

City of London

There can hardly be a square yard of the City of London that doesn't resound with history. The City has seen almost continuous human settlement since before the Romans established Londinium around 50 AD. Londinium became the fifth largest city in the Roman Empire and each modern street and building overlie other streets and buildings stretching back for nearly 2,000 years.

Lamb Tavern
10-12 Leadenhall Market
London EC3
071-626 2454
Magnificent market pub on three floors.
No-smoking bar.

A good example is Leadenhall Market, where the **Lamb Tavern** is situated. The original Leadenhall was built in 1309 by Sir Hugh Neville and had a large roof of lead (hence Leadenhall). It is uncertain whether this was built as a private dwelling or for public use but by the end of the 14th century, it seems to have been established as a market place and for some time was the City granary. The original hall was badly damaged in the Great Fire of London (1666) and the present building was designed and built by Sir Horace Jones, keeping it as a market, with a majority of butchers and fishmongers. But the site of the Lamb Tavern has much older and grander origins than a 14th-century market for it overlies the Roman basilica (a large building used for judicial and commercial purposes, many of which were later converted into churches).

The Londinium basilica was first built in about 50 AD but when the City was replanned in 120 AD, it was rebuilt as the largest building of its kind in Europe, except for the Basilica Ulpia in Rome itself. It was 500ft long (about the length of St Paul's), the eastern end lying under Leadenhall

The Lamb Tavern in 1988.

Market and the western end lying under St Peter's Church on the far side of Gracechurch Street. To the south lay the forum, with shops and workshops all around. Thus the Lamb Tavern, as a place of refreshment next to a market, is probably carrying on a tradition first established in the area by the Romans.

The Lamb is said to date from 1780 and was certainly in existence in 1806. Until it became a Young's pub in 1985, it had been independently run, although owned by the Corporation of London. In coaching days, travellers would have had bed and breakfast in the Lamb before visiting the shipping companies in Leadenhall Street to book their ocean-going passages. Famous visitors from more modern times include stars of stage and screen such as Jack Warner, Sir Richard Attenborough, Robert Mitchum, Tom Sellick, John Nettles (with all the Bergerac team) and Reg Varney (from On the Buses). The Lamb was extensively altered in 1987 and reopened with the first no-smoking bar in a Young's pub.

Fenchurch Street, where the East India Arms and Chapman's Wine Lodge are to be found, also traces its history back to the Romans. Along with Lombard Street, it was the centre of early Londinium, though Fenchurch Street may take its name from a mediaeval word for hay, derived from the French "foin"; the street of the haysellers.

East India Arms
67 Fenchurch Street
London EC3
071-480 6562
Small and often extremely busy.

Right: the East India Arms, 1988.

The **East India Arms** is named after East India House, which until 1862 stood on the site of the Lloyds Building in Leadenhall Street. It was the headquarters of the East India Company, established in 1600, which effectively came to rule India. The East India Arms, or Tavern as it was known, can be traced back to 1815. It possibly stands on the site of part of the old Lloyds Register and has been a Young's house since 1973, when it featured in an exchange deal with Bass Charrington involving the Cricketers at Richmond and became the first City pub to be run by Youngs since the Second World War.

The interior of Chapman's in 1991.

Chapman's
The Wine Lodge
Sackville House
145 Fenchurch Street
London EC3
071-626 0918
An old-fashioned pub on two floors.

Three Lords
27 The Minories
London EC3
071-481 4249
Modern pub in traditional style, on two floors.

The new Three Lords.

Chapman's, The Wine Lodge, was privately owned until taken over by Young & Co in 1986 but Young's beers were sold here as far back as 1933. The original E.A. Chapman was the tenant of the Dog and Fox, Wimbledon, in the 1930s. Wine lodges were the precursors of the modern-day wine bars and although they had full licences, they would concentrate on selling wines, ports and sherries, often on draught from casks behind the bar. Nowadays, there is more emphasis on beer at Chapman's, but sherry, port and madeira are still tapped from casks.

The **Three Lords** is around the corner in The Minories, a street named after the convent of the Little Sisters of St Clare, the Sorores Minores. Their abbey was founded in 1293 by Edmund, Earl of Lancaster, but was suppressed in 1539 during the Reformation and the church was given to the parish. The church survived until the bombs of the Second World War. The Three Lords has been rebuilt at least twice and has moved once since the first definite mention of it in 1781, when it was referred to as being in front of the Holy Trinity Church in the Minories. It is then recorded as being on its present site in 1799. By the opening of Tower Bridge in 1894, the pub had been rebuilt and redesigned and was admired by a correspondent in The City Press of

1890 for its stained glass, mosaic pavements, encaustic tiles, brilliant cut glass panels and wall decorations "on the most modern and improved principle".

The Minories today is a street of modern office blocks. The Three Lords was rebuilt in 1985 as an exact external copy of the old pub and has been leased by Youngs since 1986. During excavations for rebuilding, Roman remains were found on the site. Three wall panels inside the pub tell the story of how it takes its name from three Jacobite supporters of Bonnie Prince Charlie. It is alleged it was the custom in the pub to pledge health to "Charlie over the Border". The three lords were the Earl of Kilmarnock, Lord Lovat — a "notorious Jacobite intriguer" — and Lord Balmerino. All three were executed on Tower Hill nearby for their part in the Jacobite Rebellion of 1745.

Clapham and Wandsworth Road

Before Clapham Common was encircled with roads, it was a patch of wasteland with hillocks, ditches, ponds and grazing for sheep and cattle. Even its name means the homestead on stubby ground. Daniel Lysons, in his Environs of London (1792), says "30 years ago it was little better than a morass and the roads were almost impass-able". But owing to the "good taste and exertions of Christopher Baldring Esq . . . its present state is well known and universally admired".

Windmill
South Side
London SW4
081-673 4578
Ancient, spacious and rambling inn.
Hotel rooms.
Children's play area.
Tables outside.

The **Windmill** pub, which has stood on the Common since at least 1665, owes its name to a windmill that stood nearby. The exact location is now obscure and to confuse matters, there are also references to two windmills. A witness in a 1758 court case stated that his father remembered a windmill at Balham Wood Lane (now Nightingale Lane) transferred to the east part of the Common. It is impossible to tell whether the windmill(s) and the inn existed at the same time or whether the inn was so named after the actual mill had been demolished.

The miller, Thomas Crenshaw, is noted in the parish records in 1665 as also being an alehouse keeper, but milling must have gradually become less important and beer selling more so, and by 1789, the Windmill Inn is noted as "a very genteel and good accustomed house, many years in the possession of Mrs Simmonds". (A Companion

Above: J.F. Herring's Return from the Derby, with the Windmill in the background.
Right: the Windmill during the Second World War.

from London to Brighthelmston — J. Edwards). It also became a staging post for coaches, although Windmill Lane was still a rural track until 1840.

The Windmill Inn is pictured in J. F. Herring's print Return from the Derby, showing a lively crowd of race-goers in front of the inn, and it seems that it must have been a regular stopping point on Derby Day. The Windmill was first leased by Young & Bainbridge in 1848 and the free-hold bought in 1899. Holly Lodge, a small hotel that is now run with the Windmill, was bought by Young & Co in 1945.

The **Plough**, near Clapham Junction, was opened in 1958 to replace a pub destroyed by a bomb in 1940. The previous pub was built in 1875 by Young & Bainbridge, when they acquired the freehold, although the story goes back further, to 1701 when the original pub was built on the

Plough
89 St John's Hill
London SW11
071-228 9136
Modern pub with two bars.
Terrace garden.

Kingston Road, in what was then a small hamlet of just a few houses. There was a large oak tree in front of the pub and it is said that Dick Turpin used the pub when he was frequenting the Garratt Lane area. There is an old rhyme that commemorates the story:

Here stands the remains of the old oak tree
That flourished when the Knights of the road
*   roamed free,*
When bands of lawless yet chivalrous wights
Struck fear to the hearts of the purse proud knights.
This gay old King of the forest world,
His proud head bowed to the sun's bright smile,
His leaves to the murmuring breeze did fling.
In the cool shade of the old Plough Inn,
When Knights of the road of their deeds did sing,
As the chorus loud made the rafters ring,
They drank to the health of Turpin the bold,
When he brought to the Plough his ill gotten gold.
So here's to the memory of the old Plough Inn,
And all the memories of things that have been.

Right: the Plough in 1874.
Below left: the Plough as it was from 1875 until the Second World War.
Below right: the Plough in 1991.

The Plough in 1991, with the old brewery buildings to the right.

Plough
518 Wandsworth Road
London SW8
071-622 2777
Traditional Victorian local.

Prince of Wales
99 Union Road
London SW8
071-978 1339
A down-to-earth local.

The three Young's pubs along the Wandsworth Road have more recent origins, being part of 19th-century development from Vauxhall to Clapham.

The **Plough** in Wandsworth Road — little more than a mile from its namesake at Clapham Junction — was the tap and beer house for the Plough Brewery next door. It is not known exactly when the brewery was first established, but in 1823, Messrs Hewitt were brewers in Wandsworth Road. By 1839 they had become Hewitt & Field, although by 1874, they had moved to premises in Larkhall Lane. The Plough Brewery was owned by Woodwards from 1869 but the business was split up in 1923-24, when the freehold of the pub was bought by Youngs and the brewery buildings by Simmonds of Reading, who were later taken over by Courage. Simmonds never brewed here, however, and the site was used for bottling only until 1935. It is now used for offices.

The **Prince of Wales** was built by London County Council in 1936 in keeping with the surrounding Springfield Estate. It replaced an earlier Prince of Wales at the

The Prince of Wales before it was rebuilt in 1936 (left) and the new pub in 1940.

Surprise
16 Southville
London SW8
071-622 4623
Tiny pub in a cul de sac.
Tables outside.

same address but on a slightly different site, 80 feet south of the present building. This small pub had first been leased by Young & Bainbridge in 1859, having been built in 1846, when Union Road was new.

The **Surprise** was previously a beer house and part of working-class Victorian development of the area. The open ground nearby, Larkhall Park, is shown as a farmhouse, Lark Hall, on Rocque's map

of 1746, surrounded by fields.

It is not known when the Surprise was first built, but it may date from as early as 1839 as Southville was in existence by then, a side street of small shops and houses. The Surprise was leased by Young & Co in 1920 and the freehold was bought in 1925. It remained a beer house until the 1950s.

The Surprise in 1991.

Clapton

Lea Bridge Road was built around 1757 by order of the Lea Bridge Turnpike Act to improve the route over the River Lea from Hackney into Essex. Before this it had been Millfields Lane and was the only route into Essex in Tudor times, although carriages could not cross the river. In the 1750s, a wooden bridge was built and this was replaced with an iron bridge in 1820. It remained a turnpike road until 1872.

Prince of Wales
146 Lea Bridge Road
London E5
081-533 3463
Large two-bar pub by the River Lea.
Tables outside.

The **Prince of Wales** has long been associated with angling and during the summer months boating and bathing used to take place here. Izaak Walton, in his Compleat Angler, describes the fine sport to be had on the Lea and the abundance of flowery meadows.

The history of the pub goes back to

The Prince of Wales in 1991.

1838 when the East London Waterworks sold land and cottages to William Bradshaw. These remained cottages until the 1860s when first mention of a public house called the Prince of Wales appears. Part of the pub is now on or very near where the old turnpike house stood until 1872. The Prince of Wales was first leased by Young & Co in 1964 and the freehold acquired from Whitbread in 1990.

Claygate

Foley Arms
Foley Road
Claygate
Surrey
0372-463431
Attractive, unspoilt pub.
Garden.

The **Foley Arms** was bought by Youngs in 1888 and was probably built a few years earlier; it is not in the 1882 Kelly's Directory of Surrey but does appear in the 1887 edition. It has changed little in outward appearance since then.

The pub takes its name from the Foley family, whose arms are carved on the outside and who owned much of the land in this area of Claygate. In 1893, Young & Co conveyed a small piece of land to the Hon Fitzalan C.V. Foley for the purpose of widening Hare Lane. For many years, the pub was run as an hotel and continued to enjoy a small residential trade until the 1950s.

The Foley Arms has played an important part in the village as the adjoining Foley Hall has been used as a meeting place and for a number of activities, particularly before the village hall was built. Foley Hall is now used as a gymnasium — the headquarters of the Foley Amateur Boxing Club — and was once used by Frank Bruno for a training session.

The Foley Arms around 1920.

Clerkenwell

Sekforde Arms
34 Sekforde Street
London EC1
071-253 3251
*Small but
imposing
street-corner
local.*
Restaurant.
Tables outside.

The **Sekforde Arms** is named after Thomas Sekforde, a distinguished lawyer and patron of literature, who was the first publisher of a county atlas that came out in 1589. He retired in 1581 to Clerkenwell and died in 1588.

The Sekforde family were originally lords of the manor in Boulge, Suffolk. Sekforde Street and the pub were built between 1835 and 1840. In the middle of Sekforde Street, at the unusual address of $18\frac{1}{2}$, is the building that was once the Finsbury Bank for Savings, where Charles Dickens had an account. Perhaps he dropped into the Sekforde Arms on his way there and back.

The Sekforde Arms became a Young's pub in 1988.

*The Sekforde
Arms in 1991.*

Covent Garden

Covent Garden is named after a mediaeval garden that belonged to the Abbey or Convent of St Peter, Westminster. In 1536, the convent exchanged the garden with Henry VIII for other land and it then came into the hands of John Russell, Duke of Bedford, in two stages in 1541 and 1552. The estate was owned by the Bedfords, ever diminishing in size, until 1945 when the last parcel of land was sold. Originally, John Russell used it for pasturing his horses and building didn't start until 1630. Both Bow Street and Russell Street were built just after and soon became famous for the many coffee houses they contained.

Marquess of Anglesey
39 Bow Street
London WC2
071-240 3216
*Popular pub in the heart of
Covent Garden.*
Restaurant.

The site of the **Marquess of Anglesey** has been licensed premises, off and on, since 1663, when it was known as Edward Miles Coffee house. Directly opposite at number 1 Bow Street was the famous Will's Coffee House (also known as Wits), which was made fashionable by the poet Dryden and was visited by Pepys and Macauley and

mentioned in Fielding's novel Tom Jones. Coffee houses in Bow Street became the hub of fashionable life in the 18th century, gaining many entries in the social columns of The Tatler and The Spectator of the day. In a Russell Street coffee house, nearby, Johnson first met Boswell. Bow Street at various intervals was also known for its low characters and brothels. It was here that the Bow Street Runners first made an appearance in the fight against crime and today Bow Street police station and the magistrates' court still carry on the job.

The pub takes its name from the first Marquess of Anglesey, who lost his leg at the battle of Waterloo in 1815. The building was destroyed by bombs during the Second World War and the present pub was built in 1957. Young & Co bought the freehold in 1958 and in 1966 bought a café next door at 38 Bow Street. The pub was extensively renovated in the 1970s and extended into the old café.

The Marquess of Anglesey has seen an enormous change in trade over the years. Fashionable 17th and 18th-century coffee drinking gave way to the beer drinking of the Covent Garden fruit and vegetable traders in the 19th and 20th centuries. More recently, the closure of the market and its redevelopment as a modern shopping and entertainment centre has brought in tourists and a new daytime population working in advertising, films and design.

Croydon

Dog and Bull
24 Surrey Street
Croydon
Surrey
081-667 0877
Bustling old market pub.

The sign of the **Dog and Bull** claims that it dates from 1431 and although this cannot be proved from written record, it could be even older as parts of the Old Palace south of Surrey Street date from the 12th century and Croydon is well documented as a bustling centre of commerce since early mediaeval times. Royal permission to grant a market here was given in 1276 and the Archbishop of Canterbury lived at the Old Palace until 1758. The Dog and Bull was definitely standing by 1595, when it was called the Bell, and has always been in the thick of things, standing in a busy market street. The land at the back of the pub was originally the village pound where stray animals were kept — and possibly the animals belonging to inmates of the jail that also stood in Surrey Street. The pound continued to be used well into the second half of the 20th century. The street itself was originally known as Butchers' Row, after the dominant trade carried on there, and cattle and carcasses were kept in the Dog and Bull yard.

To one side of the Dog and Bull for many years stood a brewery, which even in 1695 was being described as "a

The Dog and Bull in the 1920s. Entire, advertised in the sign above the first floor, was a name for porter.

very ancient brewhouse". Although the owner of the brewery and the pub were not always the same, the pub probably acted as a tap room for the brewhouse over many periods of time.

One of the owners of the Dog and Bull, Nicholas Northorpe, was executed in the late 17th or early 18th century for felony. Jack Ketch, public hangman from 1663 to 1686, who was infamous for his barbarous and often botched executions (taking eight strokes to dispatch the Duke of Monmouth), is recorded as flogging an unfortunate victim through Butchers' Row from the jail to the corner of Church Street and back. It is to be hoped that Nicholas Northorpe did not also meet his fate at Ketch's hands.

Both the pub and the brewhouse changed hands many times through the 17th and 18th centuries until the Dog and Bull was leased to Young & Bainbridge in 1832. The freehold was bought in 1899, possibly the longest time it has ever been held by one family and owner. The brewery is no more, but was latterly owned by Page & Overton, until they closed in 1954. The yard is still known as Overton's Yard. The Dog and Bull was rebuilt in the 18th century and is now a Grade II listed building, possibly the oldest still standing in Surrey Street.

Croydon underwent a massive period of expansion in the 19th century and while the Dog and Bull belongs to an older period, both the **Tamworth Arms** and the **Gloucester** are products of that expansion. Two reasons for this development are the arrival of the passenger railway in 1839 and secondly, the reputation Croydon had for pure water (unlike London in the 19th century), which made Croydon seem an attractive and healthy place to live.

Tamworth Road was laid in the early part of the century, and houses were being built from about 1840 onwards. The Tamworth Arms was built between 1851 and 1855 and came into the possession of Young & Bainbridge in 1857. The freehold was bought in 1878.

The Gloucester is now a modern building, opened in 1961, built on the site of a previous Victorian beer house

Tamworth Arms
62 Tamworth Road
Croydon
Surrey
081-688 0397
Traditional old local.

Gloucester
111 White Horse Road
Croydon
Surrey
081-684 6661
Large roadside pub with a choice of bars.
Garden.

Right: the Tamworth Arms in 1920.

The Gloucester before and after rebuilding.

and then pub, which was demolished by bombs during the Second World War. Whitehorse Road, where it stands, is named after Walter Whitehorse, shield bearer to Edward III, who owned the land after 1368. The Gloucester itself probably takes its name from nearby Gloucester Lodge, which is connected to Richard III, Duke of Gloucester, who stayed in Croydon after the death of his brother to prevail upon Archbishop Bouchier to put into his care the two young princes, who later died in such mysterious circumstances in the Tower of London, leaving Richard free to become king. Thus are modern day buildings connected to important events of the past.

Dartford

Dartford is an historic market town, situated on Watling Street, the main coaching route from Dover to London, and

The Malt Shovel in the late 19th century, when it was a Truman, Hanbury, Buxton house.

Malt Shovel
3 Darenth Road
Dartford
Kent
0322-224381
Ancient and well preserved inn.
Family conservatory.
Terrace garden.

the home town of Wat Tyler. It has a number of historic buildings. In 1790, it had only 400 houses but five inns and numerous beer houses.

The **Malt Shovel** is one of many country pubs that started life as cottages. Darenth Road, formerly Short Hill, is off the main road and so would not have been involved in the coaching trade through Dartford. The oldest part of the

The Malt Shovel in 1983.

building is the tap room, which dates from 1673. There is a plaque on the wall, now covered with timber cladding, that reads "WPS 1673". The initials stand for the Christian names of the husband (W) and wife (S) and their surname (P). The tenants of these cottages probably worked in the fields nearby (Tenters Field and Paper Mill Field). The occupants in 1871 were a carpenter and his family. Possibly the tenants of the cottage started to serve beer though the windows on market day. It had become a small beer house by 1873, had become known as the Malt Shovel and is listed in the local directory of that year.

The Malt Shovel is now among Dartford's oldest buildings and is listed. It became a Young's pub in 1983.

Dorking

Dorking has ancient origins. It lies over part of the Roman road, Stane Street, and its market was claimed to be of "immemorial antiquity". Parts of Stane Street have been excavated in West Street, where the **Old House at Home** is situated.

Old House at Home
24 West Street
Dorking
Surrey
0306-889664
Full of low beams and brass.
Prize-winning garden.

The Old House at Home was originally two houses and seems to have amalgamated and become a pub some time between 1820 and 1855, when it was a fully licensed free house with two beds and three horses. The building is thought to be 14th century. Wattle-and-daub walls have been exposed, although the fascia now is turn of the century and the pub has undergone some alteration. In 1649, a survey shows a property called Banes on the site owned by

a Mr Goodwin and in the 1790s, it was occupied by the Thornton family, who were pipe makers. It has its own well in a lobby at the back.

The name of the Old House At Home comes from an early Victorian song popular with soldiers far from home and is suggestive of the Victorian origin of the building as a pub. It became a Young's house in 1989, bought from Courage.

Dulwich and Sydenham

Dulwich gets its name from an amalgam of words for dill, anise and damp meadow. Dulwich Wood Park, Wood Vale and the **Dulwich Wood House** all preserve the name of the ancient Dulwich Woode (1530). This large wood, much loved by Byron when he was a schoolboy nearby, originally covered all of the southern part of Dulwich. Today, very little of the wood remains except in these few names.

Dulwich Wood House
39 Sydenham Hill
London SE26
081-693 5666
Cosy pub with unusual features.
Large garden with pétanque.

Dulwich and Sydenham both expanded rapidly after the opening of the Crystal Palace in 1854. The Dulwich Wood House, first leased by Youngs in 1889, was possibly designed by the architect of the palace, Sir Joseph Paxton, and built in 1857 for George Ward, a local farmer. The building lease shows that development had just started when it says "situated on the South East side of the New Road through a part of Dulwich Wood called Crescent Wood Road". At first, it was the only building in the immediate area that was not owned by Dulwich College, the land having previously

Right: the Dulwich Wood House after the First World War. The building remains substantially the same today. Below: the Bricklayers' Arms, pre-1924 (left) and after rebuilding.

Bricklayers' Arms
189 Dartmouth Road
London SE26
081-699 1260
Restored corner pub with two bars.
Garden.

been sold by them. In the 1870s and 1880s the stables were used as a riding school and livery.

After the Second World War, Rex Palmer became tenant of the pub. Rex was one of the original five members of the BBC and his was the voice that for many years sang Abide with Me at the close of broadcasting on Sunday nights, as well as being Uncle Rex to the listeners of Children's Hour.

The **Bricklayers' Arms** was built in the mid 19th century and was first leased by Young & Co in 1884. The freehold was bought in 1920. The existing building dates from 1924-25, when the pub was rebuilt. During the Second World War, it was damaged six times by bombs. In 1989, the pub underwent extensive refurbishment and alterations, with a new extended back bar and redesigned garden.

East Sheen

see Mortlake and East Sheen (Page 76)

Effingham

Effingham is one of a number of Surrey Saxon villages mentioned in the Doomsday Book, built near springs or on water bearing rock. It remained a hamlet of scattered farmsteads until the 20th century, when there was a surge of building. Orestan Lane, where the **Plough** is situated, is thought to be a corruption of Western Lane; one of the local farms (now demolished) was known as Western Farm. It had also sometimes been called Brookhill Lane.

It is very likely that the Plough started life as a beer

Plough
Orestan Lane
Effingham
Surrey
0372-58121
Splendid country pub.
No-smoking area.
Garden.

An undated picture of the Plough, which hangs in the pub. The building is little changed today, except for extensions on either side.

house. There is no mention of a public house in Orestan Lane in the Kelly's Surrey Directories, even as late as 1938, although there is mention of a beer retailer. In the Victoria County History of Surrey (1911), the Plough Inn is mentioned, however. It became a Young's pub in 1989, bought from Courage.

Epsom

Epsom was first put on the map when the waters of Epsom Well were discovered in 1618. After the Restoration, it became a fashionable resort for a time. It is not known exactly when the races were established, but certainly some time between 1618 and 1648. One local historian, writing in 1901, describes Epsom as a sleepy town disturbed twice a year by the racegoers attending the Derby and the Oaks.

King's Arms
144 East Street
Epsom
Surrey
0372-723892
Traditional old pub.
Garden.

The railway came to Epsom in 1848 and the east side of the town is mainly Victorian development, although East Street, where the **King's Arms** is found, did have some 18th-century buildings in 1901.

The cellar beams in the pub are said to be from men-of-war from the Battle of Trafalgar (1805), although the first mention of the King's Arms is in Kelly's Directory of 1874. It first became a Young's pub in the 1880s and was sold to Youngs in 1908. The sale particulars from 1908 mention saloon bar, private bar, smoking room, billiard room, stables, coach-house and garden. The King's Arms was altered in 1938, when cottages next door were demolished to make way for a car park and the pub was extended, with an entrance to the garden created at the side. The lay-out of the bars was changed in 1967.

Estate agent's notice for the sale of the King's Arms and other property in 1908 and (below) the pub after the First World War.

Particulars and Conditions of Sale

OF

THE FREEHOLD

FULLY LICENSED PREMISES

KNOWN AS THE

'King's Arms' Inn,

East Street, Epsom.

LET ON A LONG LEASE AT

PER **£60** ANNUM.

11 FREEHOLD COTTAGES

With Good Gardens,

Having important Frontages to the same road of over 330 Feet.

REPRESENTING A TOTAL RENTAL OF

PER **£183 6**S. ANNUM.

A PLOT OF

Freehold Building Land

Of about 23 perches,

Which MESSRS.

LANGLANDS & SON

Will Sell by Auction, in 7 LOTS, at their

MART, HIGH STREET, EPSOM,

On WEDNESDAY, 24th JUNE, 1908,

Esher

Bear
71 High Street
Esher
Surrey
0372-469786
Beautifully restored coaching inn.
Family eating area.
Functions suite.
Tables outside.

Esher has seen some famous visitors in its time and many of them seem to have stopped at the **Bear**. The coaching route from London to Portsmouth featured the Bear as the second stop and thus often drew the famous and aristo-cratic, although throughout the 18th century it saw mainly officers on their way to and from the naval stations. Nelson stopped here on the way to Portsmouth and played bowls in the bowling alley that existed then. During Queen Mary's reign, it was a favourite place for her to wait for her hus-band, King Philip of Spain, when he landed at Portsmouth. Charles II, James II and William of Orange all used to call in on their way to Hampton Court.

The Bear's proximity to the stately home of Claremont has also brought some royal and interesting visitors. The exiled French King Louis Philippe lived at Claremont from 1848 until his death, his staff stayed at the Bear on his arrival, and for years a pair of jackboots belonging to Louis Philippe's postboy were displayed in the bar, although why he left them behind was never made clear. In 1816, Princess Charlotte and Prince Leopold of Saxe-Coburg came to live at Claremont and on moving in, they passed under a triumphal arch erected from the Bear to Nappers Corner.

The present building is mainly 18th century, although originally it was a hunting lodge owned by the Earl of Warwick, Warwick the King Maker. From this the sign is derived, as the Bear and Ragged Staff was the crest of Warwick. After Warwick's death, his butler leased the now partly dismantled lodge in about 1460 from the family and started an inn with the sign of the Bear and Ragged Staff. The Ragged Staff was removed during Henry VIII's reign after the Warwicks fell from favour and the sign was reduced to a non-rampant common bear. So it remained, apart from a short break in the 18th century when the pub was known as the Brown Bear.

Young & Co bought the Bear in 1888. In 1890, Kelly's Directory said it had been established in 1529 and added: "Coaches stop daily during the season, appointed posting house under Royal seal; stabling for 100 horses." A hundred years after it became a Young's house, in 1988, the Bear was completely renovated, with many of its original features restored.

Eton Wick

Pickwick
32 Eton Wick Road
Eton Wick
Windsor
Berkshire
0753-861713
Splendid village pub.
Tables outside.

The village of Eton Wick has Saxon origins but since 1440 it has been dominated by Eton College, which over the years has provided employment, bought produce and at one time even replaced the original parish church with the College Chapel. The provost of the college was rector of the parish and claimed a tithe from the villagers' produce, even from cottage gardens. From its origins until the beginning of the 19th century, Eton Wick was a small place: in 1841, there were only 62 houses and that was a threefold increase since the end of the previous century. But the Victorian age saw steady growth and Eton Wick Road became important as a focal point of the village.

The **Pickwick** was part of this expansion, probably being built around 1840. It first became a beer house in 1842 and was originally called the Grapes. The beer retailer, one William Simmonds, also doubled up as wheelwright (his workshop was behind the pub), carpenter, builder, grocer and coal merchant. Trade in beer was obviously a bit patchy. The name of the Grapes was changed to the Pickwick after an extension was built and general refurbishment in 1984. The pub had become rundown and it was

The Pickwick on the day Youngs took over.

decided that a new image and a new name were required. Although pictures from the Dickens novel hang inside the pub, the name was chosen because of the name of the village, to suggest that the pub is the Pick of the Wick. It became a Young's pub in 1988.

Fulham

The King's Road before the Restoration was a country lane through fields and market gardens and used only by farmers and gardeners. After 1660, it was decided to convert it to a coach road to provide a more direct route between St James's Palace and Hampton Court. It continued to be a private road for royalty, with tickets issued to commoners on sufferance until 1830. Parsons Green takes its name from a parsonage that stood on the west side of the green. The parish pound was here also.

Duke of Cumberland
235 New King's Road
London SW6
071-736 2777
Imposing and comfortable old pub with a modern public bar.

The **Duke of Cumberland** is named after Ernest Augustus, son of George III, who owned estates in the area, though the pub was for many years called the Duke's Head. Originally, it may have been the Ponds End Tavern, which had been in existence since 1657. The 1857 valuation entry in the Young & Bainbridge property book reads: "These premises were remodelled by us and improved by the transfer of the Licence of the Old Duke's Head further up the lane and badly placed." The pub, resited and presumably better placed, on the corner of Peterborough Road, was completely rebuilt by Youngs in 1894. It kept the name Duke's Head until 1971, when it took its present title after extensive refurbishment. It won the Evening Standard Pub of the Year competition the same year, and ten years later was refurbished again, with the addition of a new public bar.

The Duke of Cumberland between the wars, when it was called the Duke's Head.

The Bridge after conversion into a hotel, with the old part of the building on the right.

Greenford

Development of Greenford is almost exclusively 20th century. In 1593, it was described as "a very fertile place of corn" and in 1845, in the Home Counties Directory, as "very secluded in the bosom of the beautiful vale of Middlesex". It had a population of 588 in 1841. Until the 20th century, there were no main roads to the village at all and then a network of arterial roads and railways around London led to the rapid industrialisation and residential development of Greenford in the 1930s. In this respect the **Bridge** is typical of other developments in the area.

Land for the hotel was first leased by Young & Co in 1932, but there were many problems with the building and granting of a licence and it was not finished and opened until 1937. It was one of two licensed premises built in the area by the same developer, one to be called the Bridge and the other the Greenford. Unfortunately, the names were accidentally transposed on the licence application forms and that is why the Bridge Hotel is nowhere near a bridge, though a flyover on the A40 now runs past the building. A painting of the original bridge at Greenford now hangs at the Bridge Hotel.

Youngs bought the freehold of the Bridge in 1959, and ran it as a pub and off-licence until 1989, when it was redeveloped and 68 bedrooms added. It re-opened in May 1990 as the first of a series of hotels to be built by the brewery. The original pub has been retained alongside the hotel, with the bars restored to their former glory.

Bridge Hotel
Western Avenue
Greenford
Middlesex
081-566 6246
Three-star hotel with the old pub lovingly restored.
68 bedrooms. Restaurant.
Functions and conferences.
Tables outside.

Detail from a painting of the old bridge at Greenford, now hanging in the hotel bar.

Greenwich

Greenwich probably means "green town" and before the beginning of the 15th century was mainly known as a fishing village, although there may have been a royal residence here since the days of Edward I (1272-1307). Both Henry VIII and Elizabeth I were born at the royal palace at Greenwich and spent much time here throughout their lives. Many famous visitors have embarked at Greenwich over the years, but not all of them have been aristocratic. Greenwich was also famous for its two fairs, which attracted many ordinary Londoners. They could be rowdy affairs, and a huge number of coffee houses, taverns, beer houses and tea rooms sprang up to cater for the needs of the visitors.

Royal Hill was called Gang Lane in the 18th century, and was certainly not a respectable place. Frequented by sailors, it may have taken its name from the press gangs that roamed the streets of waterside towns looking for men to press into naval service.

The **Richard I** started life as two shops, one selling beer and the other sweets, next door to each other. Between 1920 and 1923, numbers 52 and 54 were knocked together by Tollemache & Cobbold, the Ipswich brewers who then owned the pub, and the present-day Richard I was born, although it was originally called Ye Olde House. The pub was known by many customers as the Tolly, the familiar name for the brewers, even for some years after it was bought by Youngs in 1974.

Richard I
52/54 Royal Hill
London SE10
081-692 2996
Charming two-bar local.
Garden.

The Richard I in 1991.

Ham

In Saxon, Ham simply means house or home. Land was granted in Ham and Petersham to Anne of Cleves as part of her divorce settlement from Henry VIII and she lived here for a while. Ham House, built in 1610, is the manor house although it is actually in Petersham. It is probably about Ham House that Tennyson wrote: "A Tudor chimnied bulk, of mellow brickwork on an isle of flowers." In Greater London (1895), Walford describes the village rather disparagingly: "Ham is a retired place, with a population of about 2,000. The village proper comprises a street of irregularly built common place houses, with a few of a better class and several small cottages clustering around the sides of an extensive common."

Many of these houses along the Petersham Road today are listed buildings. The **Fox & Goose** is now in a conservation area and has been designated by Richmond Council as a building of townscape merit. It is not known exactly how old the Fox & Goose is, but it was once a cider house and possibly started as a cottage selling cider through the windows on market days and holidays. It still retains a rural cottage feel, with only one bar. It is said to have a haunted cellar, with a ghostly presence being reported by the tenant and his dog, which won't go near the cellar. Objects in the pub have also been mysteriously moved around at night. Young & Co acquired the pub from Allied Breweries in 1990.

Fox and Goose
325-327 Petersham Road
Ham
Richmond-upon-Thames
Surrey
081-940 8500
Small pub with lots of character.
Garden.

Pub regulars and brewery management toast the Fox and Goose on the day it became a Young's pub in 1990.

Hammersmith

From the 15th century until the coming of the railway, Hammersmith was a market garden and brickmaking area. Until 1850, more than half the total acreage was still agricultural land. Brook Green had been described in 1813 as "a pleasant village with some good houses. An annual fair is held here on the first of May and lasts 3 days. It commands on the north good views of the surrounding country; including Harrow Church, Hampstead and Highgate". Brook Green takes its name from a small tributary of the Thames which used to run through the green. In Rocque's map of 1746, Shepherds Bush Road is called Brook Green Lane.

Brook Green
170 Shepherd's Bush Road
London W6
071-602 2643
Well restored Victorian pub.
Tables outside.

The **Brook Green**, opposite Brook Green itself, was built as a hotel in 1886, owned by the Swail family and first leased to Youngs in 1888. It was still owned by the Swails until bought by Youngs in 1944. "Improved" in the 1930s, the Brook Green has recently been restored to its late Victorian splendour with renovated wood, glasswork and decorated ceilings. In 1983, it was expanded to take in the house and shop next door at 168 Shepherd's Bush Road.

Builders
81 King Street
London W6
081-748 4511
Bustling pub with two bars.
Tables outside.

The original **Builders**, or the Builders Arms as it was called, was sited in Blacks Road, around the corner from its present site. It was leased in 1854 and bought in 1912 and when it had to be closed because of redevelopment in 1966, Youngs bought another pub called the Angel in King Street

Young's horses at the Builders in King Street in the 1960s (near right) and the Builders' Arms in Blacks Road pre-1918.

Thatched House
115 Dalling Road
London W6
081-748 6174
A popular local.
Patio.

The Thatched House between the wars (left) and in 1989.

and renamed it. The pub is now called simply the Builders, and the word Arms has been dropped.

The **Thatched House** — which has no recorded history of having been covered in thatch — was first leased in 1832 by Young & Bainbridge. A note in the property records dated 1833 records that next to the Thatched House there was "messuage adjoining formerly used as a public house but now a private house". So the Thatched House was originally next door to another pub. In 1857, the Young & Bainbridge property book notes: "These are substantial and pleasantly situated Premises let at present for £36 but well worth £50 which a succeeding tenant is to pay." The Thatched House was altered in 1878 and bought in 1899. Dalling Road was originally called Frog Lane and then Webb Lane.

The Thatched House has strong links with football through a former licensee, the former Fulham and England footballer Bedford Jezzard. He played at Craven Cottage from 1949 to 1956 and was manager of Fulham until 1964.

Hampstead

Flask
14 Flask Walk
London NW3
071-435 4580
*Well preserved pub with
two distinct bars, divided
by a magnificently
decorated screen.*
Conservatory.

*The Flask between the
wars. The present public
bar, on the corner, was
labelled Oyster Bar.*

In 1689, "six acres of waste land lying and being about certain medicinal waters called the Wells" was given by the Hon Susanna Noel on behalf of her son the Earl of Gainsborough "for the sole use, benefit and advantage of the poor of the parish of Hampstead". The land was to the east of Hampstead village and the spring ran down from the Heath to form a small natural pool. Fourteen trustees were appointed to administer the charity. By 1700, they had hit on a money-spinning idea and on 18 April of that year, they announced in The Postman that these "medicinal" waters were to be sold to the public at threepence a flask. The water was collected and taken to the **Flask** (then called the Thatched House) where it was bottled and sent by cart to London taverns and coffee houses.

The English have always had a passion for spas and mineral waters and at no time was this more true than the 18th century, which saw water become a boom industry. Hampstead quickly became fashionable in spite of some rather dubious claims for the water's properties. Scientific investigation of the time spoke of its ferruginous qualities which would benefit all whose "principal complaints were those of idleness, dissipation and frivolity". The flasks the water was sold in are now commemorated by the Flask pub and Flask Walk.

For some time, the Flask was known as the Lower Flask to distinguish it from the Upper Flask, a much grander establishment, where the Kit Kat Club met. There gathered the likes of Addison, Swift, Pope, Congreve and Sir Robert Walpole. In Samuel Richardson's novel Clarissa Harlowe (1748), the heroine takes tea at the Upper Flask, but the Lower Flask is described as "a place where second rate characters were to be found in swinish condition". The Flask flourished nevertheless and continued in its original thatched state until 1874 when it was replaced with the present building. Young & Co bought the Flask in 1904. During building work in 1990, some of the original 18th-century cellar walls were uncovered.

Horse and Groom
68 Heath Street
London NW3
071-435 3140
Elegant old pub.
Upstairs cocktail bar.

The **Horse and Groom** was also originally an 18th-century tavern and is listed in a 1721 Register of Middlesex Taverns. From 1794 to 1808 it was used for Masonic meetings by the St John's Lodge. The painter George Romney, who lived nearby at Holly Mount from 1797 until 1802, also used to visit the pub. Youngs first leased the Horse and Groom in 1889 and bought it in 1897. It was rebuilt in 1899 in the present, distinctive High Victorian style (similar to the Orange Tree at Richmond; see Page 93).

The Horse and Groom, 1920.

Harlesden

The Grand Junction Canal was built between 1793 and 1820 to link Brentford, on the Thames, to Braunston, $93\frac{1}{2}$ miles away in Northamptonshire, and so to by-pass the Oxford Canal. The Paddington arm of the canal, $13\frac{1}{2}$ miles long and added in 1801, was linked up to the Regent's Canal at Little Venice in 1831 to provide an alternative route to the Thames at Limehouse.

The canal became part of the Grand Union Canal in 1929, when the Regent's Canal Company took over a number of other canals, but the old name lives on at the **Grand Junction Arms**, alongside the Paddington arm.

Grand Junction Arms
Canal Bridge
Acton Lane
London NW10
081-965 5670
Large, traditional pub on the canalside.
Garden.

It is not known exactly when the pub was built. It is shown on the 1860 Ordnance Survey map surrounded by fields and it may have stood here since the canal was opened. Most of the land in the area was not developed until the late 19th century.

A lease of the pub was assigned to Youngs in 1892. The

The Grand Junction Arms around 1920.

lease is dated 1873 from the Company of Proprietors of the Grand Junction Arms, "the Junction Tavern, together with wharf called Lower Place Wharf". The pub originally had stables for the horses that used to tow barges along the canal, and there is still mooring for boats outside the pub. The freehold was bought by Young & Co in 1939. In 1967, land behind the pub, running alongside the canal, was exchanged with United Biscuits for land on Acton Lane, which is now the car park. In 1988, the Grand Junction Arms underwent major refurbishment and the two front bars were merged into one.

Holborn
see Bloomsbury (Page 19)

Isleworth

Coach and Horses
183 London Road
Isleworth
Middlesex
081-560 1447
Grand old pub on the main road.
Functions room.
Garden.

The **Coach and Horses** is a typical example of the coaching houses that abounded during the 17th and 18th centuries at the main stopping places along the roads into London. A Parliamentary survey of 1650 recorded 120 inns within the space of one mile on Hounslow High Street. Because they were on one of the major West Country routes, Hounslow and Isleworth saw extraordinary activity as stopping places for the 500 coaches and 1,500 horses that passed through daily. The actual date of the pub's construction is not known but it was standing in 1759 and as there were more pubs in the area in the 17th century than the 18th century, it

The Coach and Horses in 1919.

is reasonable to assume that it belongs to the 17th. In the 19th century, the coaching trade slowed down as more roads were built and the railways began to take over.

The main claim to fame of the Coach and Horses is a mention in Dickens's Oliver Twist. Oliver is taken by Bill Sykes to commit a burglary in Chertsey. After walking from Bethnal Green to Hyde Park Corner, Sykes secures them a lift in a carrier's cart to Hounslow: "As they passed the different milestones, Oliver wondered, more and more, where his companion meant to take him. Kensington, Hammersmith, Chiswick, Kew Bridge, Brentford, were all passed; and yet they went on as steadily as if they had only just begun their journey. At length they came to a public house called the Coach and Horses, a little way beyond which another road appeared to turn off. And here the cart stopped." This was Busch Corner, where the journey was continued along the Twickenham Road on foot.

Young & Bainbridge first leased the Coach and Horses in 1831 and the freehold was bought from Earl Percy, who owned Syon House and much of the surrounding land, in 1897.

Castle
18 Upper Square
Isleworth
Middlesex
081-560 3615
Large pub with two bars and a conservatory.
Family eating area.

The **Castle** was also first leased in 1831 and dates back to at least 1749. It seems to have been more associated with the growth of the village than was the Coach and Horses. The sale particulars in 1894 show that it, too, had gained trade from coaching although it was a much smaller

The Castle in the 1980s with new conservatory and the old building, which stood until the 1930s.

affair than the Coach and Horses. It had only a bar parlour and coffee room downstairs, together with a small off-licence described as a "convenient liquor shop". However, there was stabling for four horses, with two coach houses. The rent Youngs were paying before buying the Castle in 1894 was £45 a year. The Castle was rebuilt and extended in the 1930s, and a conservatory — the first of its kind at a Young's house — was added in 1987.

The Marquess Tavern, 1991.

Islington

Canonbury Street, along with Canonbury Road, Park, Place and Square are all named after Canonbury House. Once lived in by Thomas Cromwell, Goldsmith and John Dudley, Earl of Warwick, it was built for the canons of St Bartholomew in 1523 and since 1952 has been home to the Tower Theatre. Canonbury Street was laid out in 1852-56, slightly later than much of the area, as a street of small villas. Marquess Road and the **Marquess Tavern** were built at the same time. The Marquess is a good example of mid-19th-century pub architecture, with fine plasterwork ceilings and is a listed building. Youngs bought the pub in 1979 and restored it to its former glory.

Marquess Tavern
32 Canonbury Street
London N1
071-354 2975
Lovely old pub with wood panelling.
Tables outside.

The Britannia in Allen Street in the 1930s, when it was called the Britannia Brewery Tap.

Kensington

Allen Street is named after Thomas Allen, a property developer who, in 1817, promoted building in the area of Kensington between Earls Court Road and Adam and Eve Road in order to ensure some sort of unity during a time of fast speculative expansion of Kensington. Allen had been a tailor and breeches maker in Bond Street and tradition has it that his wealth came from supplying military uniforms on a huge scale during the Napoleonic wars. Allen did not build in Allen Street itself and it stayed mainly as garden ground before being developed as Wynnstay Gardens in 1893-95. It was also the home of the **Britannia** Brewery, which occupied the site of the present Allen Mansions and was built in 1834, together with the pub, by partners Edward Herington and William Wells. The top of the brewery building was dominated by a figure of Britannia looking up Allen Street. It never seems to have flourished, however. In 1873, it became known as William Wells & Co and then went bankrupt in 1902, when its only tied houses were the Britannia Brewery Tap, Allen Street, and the even smaller Britannia Stores (or Tap) in Warwick Road. The firm was set on its feet but collapsed again in 1924 and was then bought out by Young & Co.

Britannia
1 Allen Street
London W8
071-937 6905
Three-bar pub with conservatory on site of old brewery.
Tables outside.

The Britannia Brewery Tap was renamed the Britannia in 1938 and is still, in skeleton, the building of 1834, but has been much altered, mainly in 1959-60 when the lounge was extended and it was given a new front. A conservatory is now situated in the stable block of the Britannia Brewery and the outlines of the forge can still be seen on the walls.

The Britannia Tap, Warwick Road, probably in 1924.

Britannia Tap
150 Warwick Road
London W14
071-602 1649
A small but genuine local.
Garden.

The **Britannia Tap**, as the Britannia Stores is now known, was probably built as a house in 1823, when the road was known as Warwick Place. William Wells took the lease in 1889 and in 1905 it was being described as a brewery stores and beer house. It was once one of many pubs that claimed to be the smallest in London, with a bar area of only 200 square feet. It was too popular, however, and eventually had to be enlarged in 1969, thus losing claim to the title.

Kew

Kew Green has been surrounded by fine houses since the 16th century, when accommodation was needed to house visitors to the Royal Courts held at Richmond Palace and Hampton Court. Elizabeth I stayed in Sir John Puckering's house on Kew Green in 1595 and the royal connections continued when George III and Charlotte took over the Dutch House, which is now Kew Palace.

Nowadays, Kew is chiefly famous for the Royal Botanic Gardens but the village has charm and an interesting history of its own. The heart of the village around the green has changed little since the 18th century, when it was a regular venue for fairs and cricket. One match in 1737 was captained on one side by the Prince of Wales and on the other by the Duke of Marlborough. Another royal event was the marriage in 1866 of Princess Mary Adelaide and the Duke of Teck at St Anne's Church on the green.

Coach and Horses
8 Kew Green
Kew
Surrey
081-940 1208
Large pub facing the green.
Garden.

The Coach and Horses, around 1920.

The **Coach and Horses**, standing opposite the green, was first leased by Young & Bainbridge in 1831 when they took over an 1815 lease. It was one of only three inns and taverns in Kew at the time. The pub was described as "a

public house, stable, coach house, garden and appurtenances with cottage adjoining". In 1845, according to the Home Counties Directory, the tenant James Costelow was also an omnibus proprietor. In 1857, the pub was described in the Young & Bainbridge property book as "pleasant and thriving premises". The Coach and Horses then, as it is now, was at the heart of village life, doing a busy trade. The freehold was bought in 1898.

There is an interesting link between the Coach and Horses and the history of photography. In 1827, Joseph Niepce (a Frenchman) came to stay at the pub while looking for funding from George IV via the Director of the Royal Botanic Gardens. Niepce had actually produced a primitive photograph in 1816, 23 years before Fox Talbot. He wrote to his children from the Coach and Horses: "Our hosts are very nice people but the meals are bad and the beds worse and it is very expensive. It costs us for your mama and me over 100 francs (then £4) for board and lodging." This was, of course, before Youngs took over.

Kilburn

Kilburn High Road was once part of the Roman road, Watling Street, and Kilburn takes its name from a bourn, or brook, that rises in Hampstead, runs through and lends its name to Marylebone and Tyburn, and is now covered and used as a drain.

Writing in Old and New London at the end of the 19th century, Walford remarks: "Such [is] the progress of bricks and mortar in swallowing up all that was once green and sylvan in this quiet suburb of the metropolis that the village of Kilburn, which within the last fifty years was still famous for its tea-gardens and its mineral spring, has almost become completely absorbed into that vast and still increasing City."

Queen's Arms
1 High Road
London NW6
071-624 5735
Modern pub with three bars.
Roof garden.
Tables outside.

The **Queen's Arms** was first leased by Young & Bainbridge in 1839, in an unfinished state, the lease stipulating that the pub was to be finished with the year. Young & Bainbridge ensured it was, although the freehold of the pub was not bought by Young & Co until 1980. By 1857, Young & Bainbridge were leasing out the stables of the Queen's Arms to the London General Omnibus Company, whose omnibuses were drawn by horses.

The Queen's Arms was once one of a string of pubs run by flashy Victorian pub entrepreneurs, the brothers Richard

Right: The Queen's Arms in the 1920s. Note the steam delivery vehicle at the side of the pub.
Below, left: all that was left after the pub was bombed in the Blitz.
Below right: the rebuilt pub, with a new forecourt lay-out, pictured in 1989.

and William Baker. On a lease from Young & Co, Richard's wife Emily became the landlady of the Queen's Arms. With money made from buying and selling pubs, the Bakers became aristocrats in the public house world and owned many sites around Leicester Square. The Baker brothers are also credited with having introduced electricity into the Victorian pub in the late 1880s. The Bakers assigned their interest in the Queen's Arms in 1898. The pub was altered in 1928 but unfortunately destroyed by a bomb in 1940. It was rebuilt and reopened in 1958.

Kingston-upon-Thames

Kingston claims, along with Winchester, to be the ancient capital of England. The Anglo-Saxon kings were crowned within its walls, hence its name, Kings Town. A market has been held here since mediaeval times and there are some 16th-century buildings still standing. Three of the Young's pubs in Kingston are products of Victorian development, however, and the other is completely modern.

Grey Horse
46 Richmond Road
Kingston-upon-Thames
Surrey
081-546 4818
Town centre local.
Live music.

Albert Arms
57 Kingston Hill
Norbiton
Kingston-upon-Thames
Surrey
081-546 7669
*Imposing pub with many
traditional bars.*
Tables outside.
Patio garden.

The **Grey Horse** is the oldest and was built in 1849. It was originally owned by George Nightingale, brewer at the local Nightingale's Steam Brewery and Mayor of Kingston in 1846. The brewery and its four pubs were sold in 1891. Young & Co took over the Grey Horse but the brewery buildings were bought by Kingston Corporation and demolished for the borough's first council housing scheme.

The Grey Horse, around 1920.

The **Albert Arms** was bought by Youngs in 1886. It was built in 1855 and named after Prince Albert. Land surrounding the pub was largely brickfields, with a few large houses on Kingston Hill. The story goes that would-be inmates of the old Kingston Workhouse, now Kingston Hospital, opposite the pub would bury small amounts of money in the roadside verges, now part of the pub car park, in order to gain admittance to the workhouse by claiming destitution.

The pub was altered in 1894-95 and again in the 1930s. When Kingston Hill was the main route from London to Kingston, before the by-pass was built, the Household Cavalry used to stop here for refreshment for both men and horses on their way from Buckingham Palace to Windsor. It is said that Edward VII, when he was Prince of Wales, also occasionally stopped here on his way to Windsor. The Albert Arms was completely refurbished in 1988.

*The Albert Arms, shortly
after the First World War.*

The Spring Grove, around 1920.

Spring Grove
13 Bloomfield Road
Kingston-upon-Thames
Surrey
081-549 9507
*Fine old pub with two
distinct bars.*
Garden.

The **Spring Grove** gets its name from the Spring Grove Estate, 11 acres of farm and meadow land which also took in the grounds of the Grove mansion, now the site of Kingston Polytechnic. This land was divided for building plots in 1866. The Spring Grove was built in 1867, Bloomfield Road having been laid out the previous year. Young & Co first took a lease in 1896 and bought the pub in 1922. The Spring Grove has changed very little since 1867 and retains the original facade.

Bishop Out of Residence
2 Bishop's Hall
off Thames Street
Kingston-upon-Thames
Surrey
081-546 4965
*Modern riverside pub with
a traditional interior.*
Tables outside.

In contrast, the **Bishop Out of Residence** was built and opened in 1979 on the site of an old tannery. Unusually, it was named by a Young & Co shareholder after the brewery chairman had requested names for the new pub at the company's annual general meeting. The name refers to the Bishop's Palace, built on the riverside here for William de Wykeham (1376 to 1404).

*The Bishop Out of
Residence, 1991.*

Lambeth

see Clapham and Wandsworth Road (Page 33)

Lee

"A short walk [from Eltham] brings us to the rapidly increasing village of Lee, the principal part of which is built on the rising ground sloping up towards Blackheath. Since the formation of the branch line of the North Kent Railway through the parish, a considerable increase has been made in the number of dwellings." So writes Walford in his Old and New London at the end of the 19th century. He goes on to say that Lee "has become of late years a favourite place of residence for City merchants and men of business and every available plot of ground has been covered with terraces of detached and semi-detached villas".

To attract this expanding trade, the **Crown** was rebuilt in 1877 from an earlier pub and sale particulars in 1882 describe it rather grandly as the Crown Hotel, "a fully licensed free house hotel". Before long, however, it was just the Crown Tavern and in 1885, leased to a brewer, Arthur Charles Morgan. The origin of Burnt Ash is unknown and may be derived from charcoal manufacture in the extensive woodland that used to exist here. In the 1880s, Corona Road was new and the Crown had detached stables on land behind the pub on Corona Road. The pub seems then to have passed through several hands, possibly an indication that trade wasn't quite what had been expected when the "hotel" was built, before being taken over in 1896 by Youngs. It was altered in 1897 and went back to being described as an hotel.

The freehold of the Crown was bought by Young & Co in 1971. It was substantially altered in 1973-74 and in 1977 the council closed part of Corona Road, which has since been included in the pub's car park.

Crown
117 Burnt Ash Hill
London SE12
081-857 6607
Imposing suburban pub.
Patio.
Functions room.

The Crown, decorated for the Coronation of King George VI and Queen Elizabeth in 1937.

Loughborough Junction

see Camberwell (Page 23)

Mayfair

Mayfair gets its name from a cattle market first authorised by James II in 1686 and always held in the first two weeks of May. It was suppressed in 1730 when gentlemen's residences were beginning to grow around it. Until development started in the 1720s and 30s, the land had been fields on the Berkeley Estate but by the late 18th century, it had all been built over. Berkeley Square was built in the 1730s and Bruton Street around 1727. It was named from Lord Berkeley's Dorset Estate, as were many of the other place names in the area.

Guinea
30 Bruton Place
Berkeley Square
London W1
071-409 1728
A small country-style pub in the bustle of Mayfair.
Restaurant.
Board room for functions.

The **Guinea** was first leased by Youngs in 1888. The name is interesting, sometimes being shown as One Pound One, the value in £sd of a guinea. However, the guinea coin was introduced in the 17th century, after the Restoration, so this earlier name is the only evidence to support the claim that the pub dates back to the 15th century.

Bruton Place had originally been called North Bruton Mews and was the mews for the north side of Bruton Street. It was built as additional stabling accommodation.

The first mention of the Guinea is in 1755, though it may also have been known as the Running Horses, the Duke's Head or the Duke of Cumberland for a time. The Guinea would have catered for the servants and stable hands of the owners of the large houses in Bruton Street and Berkeley Square. It is now mainly an early 19th-century building. In 1953, a restaurant was added and has become renowned for its steaks and is immensely popular with American visitors.

The Guinea between the wars.

The Windmill on the day it became a Young's house in 1990.

It has had many famous guests over the years: Princess Margaret, Richard Burton, Elizabeth Taylor, Charlton Heston, Jack Nicklaus, Frank Sinatra and King Hussein among them.

Mill Street is named after a mill that used to stand near Hanover Square, and Conduit Street preserves the memory of a conduit that stood in the middle of Conduit Mead, a large field on which New Bond Street and its immediate neighbours were built. This field was the meeting place for hunts in the 16th century, as Stowe records in his Survey of London (1582). In the 18th and 19th centuries, Mill Street contained pubs that catered for the coachmen and stable hands of the large houses nearby.

Windmill
6-8 Mill Street
London W1
Bustling pub in a side turning off Conduit Street.
Restaurant.

The **Windmill** is a Victorian building. In 1842, the site was houses and shops, occupied by tradesmen. Nearly 150 years later, it was trading as a night-club called the Topaz until turned into a public house by Mr Michael Shiel in 1988. He sold his lease to Youngs in 1990.

Merton

King's Head
18 High Street
London SW19
081-540 7992
Large, two-bar pub.
No-smoking area.
Function room.
Tables outside.

Between 1117 and 1538, there was a priory at Merton founded by the Augustinian order, which became rich and influential under Royal patronage. Henry VI and his court spent time here in the 15th century. Like most priories of the time, Merton would have brewed its own beer and if the **King's Head** does date from 1496 as it claims, then it could have been built to sell off the surplus beer the priory was brewing and to act as an hospice for travellers. One auth-

The King's Head, before it was rebuilt in 1931.

ority believes an inn has stood here since 1594, perhaps taking over the hospitality traditionally associated with the priory after the Dissolution.

There is an interesting link with the history of Epsom, for after the waters of Epsom were discovered in 1618 and Epsom became fashionable, a daily post from Epsom to London was started in 1684, stopping at Merton and linking Merton to London for the first time. The coaches almost certainly would have stopped at the King's Head.

Although still a small village, Merton was only an hour's drive away from London and in the 17th and 18th centuries, the King's Head continued as the inn from which the daily coach service ran. In 1801, Nelson bought Merton Place, having longed for a retreat in the country. He lived at the house with Lord and Lady Hamilton in a curious menage à trois. The house cost £9,000 and Nelson's move into the district immediately put up other property prices. Nelson would often have hired a post chaise from the King's Head for the journey to and from London and when he set off to sea in 1805 for the last time before the Battle of Trafalgar, he wrote in his diary: "Friday night at half past ten, drove from dear, dear Merton where I left all that I hold dear in the world to go and serve my King and country".

In 1808, Emma Hamilton sold Merton Place and the estate was broken up. The house stood empty until the railway came to Merton in 1838 and brought with it a flood of suburban housing. Merton Place was demolished.

The character of Merton was soon changed forever with increasing industrialisation and building but the King's Head remains, although it, too, has changed. Young &

Prince of Wales
98 Morden Road
London SW19
081-542 0573
Traditional old pub on main road.
Garden.

Bainbridge first bought a lease of it in 1831 and the freehold was bought in 1899. It was rebuilt in 1931 with a new fascia.

In 1824, a piece of farmland known as Fouracres Meadow on the London Turnpike Road was sold at auction for £62 and on this the **Prince of Wales** was built, though the exact date is obscure. Several cottages were built immediately behind the pub on what became Avenue Terrace.

Young & Bainbridge first took a lease of the Prince of Wales in 1876 and Youngs bought the freehold in 1919. The draymen always had great difficulty delivering beer to the Prince of Wales because of the narrow road and because they were not allowed to turn round in the entrances to properties behind the pub. So, in 1949, after the houses had been destroyed by wartime bombing, Youngs bought the land. Externally, the Prince of Wales has changed very little and retains its mid-Victorian frontage.

Mitcham

Sir Walter Raleigh and John Donne both had houses at Mitcham. The land around was largely occupied by physic gardens and Lysons comments in Environs of London (1792) that he knew no other place that had such a large acreage planted with herbs. Roses, camomile, white poppies, liquorice, peppermint, angelica and lavender were all grown in large quantities — although the impression of gardens perhaps belies the fact that those parts of Mitcham around the Wandle were industrialised from an early time. However, even today it retains a village atmosphere.

Mitcham is famous in the annals of cricket and the Mitcham XI were among the best known provincial clubs in

The Cricketers in 1919.

Cricketers
340 London Road
Mitcham
Surrey
081-648 1460
A modern pub with two bars.
Garden.
Restaurant.

the days of George III. Both the ground and the club at Mitcham claim to be the oldest in the world, with the first recorded mention of the game in the village being in 1685.

Although different in style and appearance, the Young's pubs in Mitcham have all been serving Young's beers since the 1830s.

The **Cricketers** commemorates cricketing connections, both in its name and the display of memorabilia inside. The earliest evidence of the pub is 1789. In a 1803 lease, however, it is called the White Swan — the same name as another pub nearby — but it had become the Cricketers by 1823. Young & Bainbridge first leased the pub in 1831 and bought it in 1881. A famous and popular cricketing pub, it

All that was left of the Cricketers after it was hit by a bomb in the 1940s.

was the headquarters of the Mitcham club, providing a meeting place, dressing rooms and a raised balcony for the scorers. The pub was run by the former England cricketer James Southerton from 1875 until his death in 1880.

In the late 19th century, in the first days of the Australian tours, the Australian team spent time training here. The original pub was unhappily demolished by a bomb during the Second World War and for many years a temporary hut was used as a makeshift pub until the present building was opened in the 1950s by the Bedser twins, Alec and Eric.

The **Bull** has been in existence since at least 1780 when it was sometimes referred to as the Black Bull. The 1780 lease mentions other documents going back to 1703, but whether this was for the land before the pub was built is not clear. In 1780, it seems to have been part of, or bordering

Bull
32 Church Road
Mitcham
Surrey
081-648 1554
Small and friendly local.
Club room.
Garden.

Church Lane at the end of the 19th century, with the Bull in the centre.

on, a farm house and yard and it was leased to the farmer. Edwards, in his Companion from London to Brighthelmston (1789), says as one leaves the green "on the right is the Black Bull, a genteel and good accustomed public house kept by Mr Sanders". It was first leased by Young & Bainbridge in 1832 and bought by Young & Co in 1899. It has changed little in appearance since the 19th century.

King's Arms
260 London Road
Mitcham
Surrey
081-648 0896
*Imposing town-centre pub
with two bars.*

The **King's Arms** was first leased in 1837 and bought in 1885, although it is mentioned in the Parish Records of 1787. When it was bought by Young & Co in 1885, the pub offered "private and public bars, Bar Parlour, Smoking Room . . . Yard in the rear with detached Stable Building for 2 Horses, Coach House and Loft Over". As the picture below shows, the pub was then timber built and typical of the area. The two shops next door were also bought, one of which was a butchers and slaughterhouse. These were demolished in 1899 when the pub was rebuilt and the road layout altered. The pub was altered again internally in 1935.

Left: the King's Arms in the late 19th century. The name of the licensee, a Mr Gould, prominently displayed over the door, dates the picture between 1885 and 1895. Below: The King's Arms is behind the horse and cart in this view from the same period. The pub was rebuilt in 1899-1900 and now stands at the junction of London Road and Merton Road, where the chestnut tree is in the picture.

Mortlake and East Sheen

Mortlake, like its close neighbour Barnes, is an ancient village on the Thames. The Doomsday Survey shows that the old manor of Mortlake was large and included the parishes of Mortlake, Wimbledon, Barnes and Putney. The manor house in Mortlake became the occasional residence of the Archbishops of Canterbury. Like Battersea, the village became famous for its beds of asparagus but these were built over in the late 19th century. In 1821, Mortlake had 403 houses and in 1839, it was described in Robson's Commercial Directory as "an improving and healthy village on the Thames . . . its neighbourhood is the residence principally of the higher circles."

Jolly Gardeners
36 Lower Richmond Road
London SW14
081-876 1721
Traditional pub surrounded on three sides by Watney's brewery.
Garden.

The first mention of the **Jolly Gardeners** is as the Three Tuns in 1720. The present name, which appeared in 1796, is possibly a reference to the expanding market gardens of the area. Jolly was an 18th-century means of expressing a trade — just as Arms came to be used in the same way in the 19th century. Young & Bainbridge first leased the Jolly Gardeners in 1833 and the property book records: "This is a snug roadside house which has been almost rebuilt by us." By the 20th century, however, trade had expanded and the old pub was felt to be too small. It was rebuilt in 1922. In 1987, during major renovations and refurbishment, the screen separating the public and saloon bars was removed.

The Jolly Gardeners before and after it was rebuilt in 1922.

Charlie Butler
40 High Street
London SW14
081-878 2310
Modern building opposite Watney's brewery.
Tables outside.

The **Charlie Butler** was opened by Youngs in 1968 to replace an earlier pub called the Old George, which was demolished for road widening, and is probably the only pub ever to be named after a brewery employee — Charlie Butler, head horsekeeper at Youngs for 43 years.

Charlie was born in Lincolnshire in 1899 and left home at 15 to work for the famous Shire stud in Nottingham owned by Forshaws, where his uncle had been stud groom

Top left: the Old George around 1920. Top right: the Charlie Butler, which replaced it in 1968. Right: the pub sign depicting Charlie Butler with one of his horses, Steve.

for 40 years. He joined Young & Co when he was 24 to help start up the show stable and he began Young's association with black Shires. Over the years that Charlie was with Youngs, the show horses won more than 3,000 first prizes and championships at shows throughout England. He retired in 1966 and died in 1980.

The horse in the pub sign with Charlie is Steve, then 23 years old. The sign was painted by Michael Francis, RA.

East Sheen in the 18th and 19th centuries was practically a hamlet of Mortlake. The **Hare and Hounds** dates from at least 1776, when East Sheen was very much a rural backwater between Putney and Richmond, with a handful of large houses and estates dotted along the Richmond Road. A pack of hounds was kept in the neighbourhood, according to the particulars of the sale in 1776 of Palewell, a large estate nearby, and this may be the origin of the name.

The Hare and Hounds was first leased by Young &

Hare and Hounds
216 Upper Richmond Road West
London SW14
081-876 4304
Large, rambling pub with a choice of bars.
Garden.

The Hare and Hounds in the 1920s.

Bainbridge in 1831 and had extensive grounds with lawns and kitchen gardens on the other side of Church Walk. Young & Co bought the freehold in 1897 and two years later, the large kitchen gardens were exchanged for land from the Hollies, a grand residence next to the pub. The Hollies was set in more than an acre of gardens, with eight bedrooms, a library, conservatory, carriage drive and coach-houses. Its lodge, Holly Lodge, was bought by Young & Co in 1902 and demolished. The rest of the grounds was sold for building development. The pub then expanded its frontage on the Upper Richmond Road.

The Railway Bell before the Second World War.

Norwood

Norwood is literally North Wood and until the beginning of the 19th century, was relatively cut off from the rest of what is now South London because of the lack of proper or passable roads. At the end of the 19th century, Walford describes it in Old and New London as "a village scattered round a large wild common". As late as 1802, a hermit was said to be living in the woods. The area was popular with

The Hope, around 1920.

Railway Bell
14 Cawnpore Street
London SE19
081-761 4521
*Back-street local restored
on traditional lines.*
Garden.

Hope
49 High Street
London SE27
081-670 2035
Small, friendly local.

gypsies and purported to be their headquarters (hence near-by Gipsy Hill). Modern Norwood dates from 1806, when the landowner, Lord Thurlow, died. All his land in Lambeth and Streatham was sold in 1810. After the railway arrived in 1856, growth was rapid.

The two Young's pubs in Norwood are both mid-Victorian beer houses.

The **Railway Bell,** bought by Young & Co in 1885, had been built in 1865. It won the Evening Standard Pub of the Year competition in 1981.

The **Hope** was first leased in 1850 and was probably built at this time. It was bought in 1902 and remained a beer house until after the Second World War.

Oxford

The history of the university at Oxford is said to go back to 727 when a convent was set up by St Frideswide and 12 of her friends, starting a monastic foundation that became known for religious teaching together with the elements of grammar and written language. These schools were restored by King Alfred and were the forerunners of the modern colleges. The site of the **King's Arms** and Wadham College was once a religious house run by the Augustinian Friars and after the Dissolution, the land was bought by the city. In 1610, it was sold to Dorothy Wadham for the purpose of establishing Wadham College. The King's Arms was not at that time part of the sale but was acquired by the college at a later date.

The King's Arms was opened on 18 September 1607,

King's Arms
40 Holywell Street
Oxford
0865-242369
*Large, imposing city-centre
pub on the corner of Parks
Road; several contrasting
bars.*
Restaurant.

when a licence was granted to Thomas Franklin, "a man of honest fame and reputation and of competent wealth and ability to keep an inn at his dwelling house . . . called the Austin Friars, a very necessary, fit and convenient house to be used for an inn, both in respect of the situation thereof, having back gates and many commodious rooms with good and sufficient furniture, fit for receiving, lodging, harbouring and entertaining of guests, and plenty of stable room for horses, and a very large Court, or backside, for the safe receipt and safe custody and keeping of carts, wains and other goods".

The King's Arms later became popular for the performance of plays and in the courtyard of the inn, the first performance of Hamlet was given in Oxford by a group of visiting players. The practice was halted during the days of the Cromwells, but became popular again after the Restoration, with plays being put on every day at the inn.

Today, the King's Arms is a large pub, with five bars, consisting of two buildings that have merged, one partly 17th century, the other 18th century. The Dons' Bar, which has fine mullioned windows, and the snug, which until relatively recently were for men only, have a separate entrance from Holywell Street and are possibly the oldest part. The

The King's Arms on the day it became a Young's house in 1991. Left: the front of the building at the corner of Holywell Street and Parks Road. Right: the Dons' Bar.

King's Arms, a grade II listed building, has long been a favourite haunt of both the academic and sporting worlds. It became a Young's house in January 1991 on a long lease from Wadham College.

Oxshott

Oxshott (or Ockshott as it appears in Victorian entries) was a small hamlet, considered to be part of Stoke D'Abernon until 1915. The Licensed Victuallers' Records show a Bear at Stoke D'Abernon in 1822, run by John Arters. He is also listed as having a licence in Stoke D'Abernon in 1816, so we may assume that this was the **Bear**, although the pub names are not listed. This is the earliest written record.

Bear
Leatherhead Road
Oxshott
Surrey
0372-842747
Comfortable country pub on the main road.
Restaurant.
Conservatory.
Garden.

In 1845, Stoke D'Abernon and Oxshott had only 382 inhabitants between them and no pub or beer retailer. It may be that the Bear lost its licence for a while for it is listed in Kelly's 1855 Surrey Directory as still one of only a handful of buildings.

Youngs bought the Bear from Courage in 1989.

Right: The Bear after it was taken over by Youngs in 1989.

Peckham Rye

Peckham started life as a small village around a common, famous for its fair. The 1839 Robson's Commercial Directory has under the entry for Peckham: "The most prominent object is the Licensed Victuallers' Asylum for 101 decayed members of that occupation." The asylum had been opened in 1827. Building over the original common started in the middle of the 19th century and Peckham has since been engulfed by the southwards expansion of London. To the south of Peckham Village, Peckham Rye Park was formed from fields in 1894.

Clock House
196a Peckham Rye
London SE22
081-693 2901
Comfortable pub decorated with many clocks.
Tables outside.

The **Clock House** was a shop in Victorian times and at some stage it became an off-licence, owned and run by the Paine family, who also ran another off-licence at Earlsfield that was to end up as a Young's pub (see Halfway House,

Outside and inside the Clock House in the 1990s.

Page 131). In 1939, H.A. Paine sold the Peckham Rye business, by now called the Clock House, to the London Off-Licence Company. When Young & Co took over this company in 1962, it was realised that the site was ideal for a pub. A full on-licence was granted in 1969 and by 1970, it had been converted into the Clock House pub. The name comes from the Victorian clock built under the gables of the original shop and the clock theme has been continued inside the pub.

Pimlico

Millbank is named after a water mill belonging to the Abbey of St Peter of Westminster that stood until the mid-17th century at the junction of Millbank and Great College Street. Although it is hard to believe now, Millbank was a

The Morpeth Arms, 1991.

Morpeth Arms
58 Millbank
London SW1
071-834 6442
Lovingly restored pub in a Regency terrace.
Restaurant/functions room. Tables outside.

Rising Sun
46 Ebury Bridge Road
London SW1
071-730 4088
Modern, single-bar pub.
Tables outside.

The 1891 Rising Sun (left) and the 1961 version.

notorious slum and no-go area before 19th-century slum clearance created the river frontage we know today.

The Tate Gallery, the illustrious neighbour of the **Morpeth Arms**, was opened in 1897 on the site of the Penitentiary, an early 19th-century prison based on a design by the philosopher Jeremy Bentham in an octagonal shape, his Panopticon. Although demolished in 1890, it acquired enough of a reputation during its 80-odd years to strike fear into the heart of anyone destined to be confined there. Barges were towed on the Thames nearby to take prisoners to the ocean-going ships that ultimately transported them to Australia.

The Morpeth Arms is said to be haunted by the ghost of a prisoner who tried to tunnel his way out of the Penitentiary to escape being transported and ended up lost in the labyrinth of vaults beneath the pub. Some visitors to the vaults are said to have felt a hand tapping them on the shoulder and a presence that drips water on them.

The pub is named after the chief commissioner responsible for the redevelopment of the area, Viscount Morpeth. It was built in 1845 by Paul Dangerfield, who specialised in pubs, and was originally kept by William Dangerfield, who may have been his brother. It is now Grade II listed and first became a Young's pub in 1984, when it was completely refurbished.

The **Rising Sun** was one of the few Young's pubs leased in 1832 that were sited north of the river. The original lease is dated 1827 and Ebury Bridge Road was called Commercial Road until around 1915. The 1857 valuation entry in the Young & Bainbridge property book notes: "These premises are held on a Lease of 58¼ years at a Rent of £100 per annum but are let at only £50 per annum. They

The Royal Oak on the day it opened as a Young's pub in 1989.

Royal Oak
1 Regency Street
London SW1
071-834 7046
Traditional street-corner pub.
Functions room.

Fountain
Station Road
Plumpton Green
Lewes
East Sussex
0273-890294
Picturesque village local.
Garden.

are large, commodious and substantial. The trade is not as large as it might be with a more courteous tenant. It is intended to ask £75 per annum from the next Tenant but more can hardly be expected unless New Westminster or Pimlico Suspension Bridge cause a great increase of traffic". Presumably trade did improve for Young & Co renewed their lease and rebuilt the Rising Sun in 1891. This building was damaged by bombs in 1942. The pub was patched up but even before the war it had been felt that it was too small. It became rather run down and this, together with the demolition of the house next door at number 44, prompted the decision in 1955, with permission from Grosvenor Estates, who own the site, to rebuild the Rising Sun yet again. The present building was opened in 1961, taking in the site of number 44 as well.

In 1981, there was more damage at the Rising Sun when an IRA bomb was detonated in an army bus outside the pub. All the windows, save one, were broken but no major damage was caused. The Prime Minister, Mrs Margaret Thatcher, visited the Rising Sun to see the damage for herself.

The pub was enlarged and improved in 1988, with the two bars being merged into one.

The **Royal Oak** became a Young's pub in 1989. Regency Street was built as part of improved approaches to Vauxhall Bridge, was opened by the Prince Regent in 1811 and was originally called Regent Street. The Royal Oak is listed in the 1842 London Directory. There is no reason to believe that it did not form part of the original development of the area of 1811, although it now has the date 1872 on one side, probably referring to a date of rebuilding.

Plumpton Green

Plumpton might be more famous for its racecourse now, but at the beginning of the 20th century, the village was renowned for hare-coursing. Even earlier, it was known for its apples. In 1801, the population was 229 and in 1851, around the time the **Fountain** was built, it was still only 353.

The Fountain in 1989.

The Fountain, Young's only pub in Sussex, has its origins in a bakehouse. The first mention of a public house is in 1879, sited next to the bakehouse, but as the occupier of the premises was a beer retailer, it is probable that beer was being sold here before 1879. For a time, the two businesses were carried on by the owner, Mr George Norman, brewer of Cooksbridge. Norman's tenant sublet one of the rooms at the Fountain to a shoemaker who also carried out his business on the premises for more than 12 years. In 1899, the Fountain Inn passed out of the Norman family to Tamplin's Brewery of Brighton. Young & Co bought the pub in 1965.

Putney

As Putney is so near to the brewery in Wandsworth, it is perhaps not surprising that Youngs have maintained a strong presence here since 1831. The five Youngs pubs were originally leased from the Tritton family in the early 1830s after the brewery had been sold to Young & Bainbridge. This seems a strong indication that they had all previously been Tritton pubs and thus have a connection with the brewery that is older than the Young family's own.

There has been a village at Putney since at least the Doomsday Survey and probably long before. Edwards, in his Companion from London to Brighthelmston, calls it "one of the pleasantest villages near London, having many fine houses". For a small place, retaining its rural character until the 19th century, it has seen a surprising number of illustrious visitors. Thomas Cromwell, Henry VIII's Lord High Chancellor, was born here. His father, Walter, had a small brewery and smithy in Putney and it has been

The Green Man pictured on a postcard dated 1905.

Green Man
Putney Heath
London SW15
081-788 8096
Country-style pub on the
edge of the heath.
Garden.

suggested by several historians that this was on the site of the present **Green Man**. The earliest that the present building can be traced to is around 1700, although some old maps show an earlier pub on the site called the Anchor.

In 1647, Oliver Cromwell, a relation of the Putney Cromwells, stationed his New Model Army at Putney and it was in the 17th century that Putney became popular. Pepys records visiting to view the young ladies and going to church at Putney. About this time, Putney Heath, on the edge of which the Green Man stands, became a noted duelling spot. In May 1652, Lord Chandos killed Colonel Compton. In 1667, the Duke of Buckingham killed, with a sword stroke, the Earl of Shrewsbury in a duel over Shrewsbury's wife. William Pitt and Tierney duelled in 1798 over a Parliamentary bill, although honour was satisfied after both parties had fired twice and missed. Castlereagh and Canning met here in 1809: Castlereagh's life was saved by a button on his coat but Canning was wounded in the leg. One can imagine the contestants and their seconds retiring to the Green Man for a stiff drink (and first aid) after these high dramas.

Putney Heath also became notorious for highwaymen and a rumour existed during the 19th century that Dick Turpin himself had hidden his guns in an upstairs room at the Green Man. Other robbers used the tap room to watch their victims taking refreshment in the parlour bar before going after them when they resumed their journey across the Heath. A famous literary visitor was the poet Swinburne, who lived in Putney. The Green Man became one of his regular stopping places and the chairs he and his friends used are still there today.

Young & Bainbridge first leased the pub in 1831 and the 1857 property book records: "These premises are held from year to year. They do a very good trade and yield about as much Rent as we pay. We should regret to lose them but can hardly [give] any actual value to such a tenancy." The freehold was bought in 1931.

Castle
220 Putney Bridge Road
London SW15
081-788 0972
Modern building with two traditional bars.
Large paved garden.
Restaurant.

The **Castle** was originally the Castle Inn and its first written mention occurs in 1758, when it is recorded as being used for Masonic meetings by the Britannic Lodge from 1758 to 1764. Young & Bainbridge took over an 1820 lease of the pub in 1831. The Castle Inn was a small single-bar roadside pub and from the 1880s onwards, Young & Co bought the leases and freeholds of the neighbouring cottages in Brewhouse Lane in order to expand the pub.

The old Castle was demolished in 1935 for rebuilding, but the new pub had been standing for only three years when it was destroyed by a bomb on 19 April 1941, with the loss of 53 lives, and for some years, customers were served from a temporary hut until the new pub could be built. The present building was opened in 1959.

Putney was once the home of the Earl of Essex, the favourite of Queen Elizabeth I; his house, Essex House,

The old Castle, which was demolished in 1935.

The Spotted Horse in 1920 (left) and in the 1940s.

Spotted Horse
122 Putney High Street
London SW15
081-788 0246
Mock-Tudor building with a spacious interior.

Duke's Head
8 Lower Richmond Road
London SW15
081-788 2552
Magnificent riverside pub with ornate glass and woodwork.

was in the High Street, which had a quite different character then, with large houses fronting the street and lawns and gardens at the back. In 1817, four large houses were still standing — the Lawn, Garden House, Fairfax House and Essex House — but the rest of the High Street was already built up.

The **Spotted Horse** was originally called the Blue Anchor and the first mention of the present name was in 1754. The sign, a carved wooden black and white spotted horse is very unusual but seems to belong to the 20th century since it does not appear in early photographs of the pub.

The Spotted Horse was first leased by Young & Bainbridge in 1832. The 1857 property book records: "This is a small substantial brick built House in the High Street let at £48 per annum". The building was altered in 1877 and bought in 1899. In the 1940s, the Spotted Horse was where the British traitor Fuchs divulged atomic research secrets to his KGB contact.

The **Duke's Head** was also first leased by Young & Bainbridge in 1832 as "a public house with the large assembly tea or club room and the tea gardens". The 1857 property book records: "This is an old well accustomed Waterside House. It is let at £50 per annum yielding an Improved Rent of £15 10s for 7³⁴ years." In 1864, the pub was rebuilt and again altered in 1894. The freehold was bought in 1899. The discus skittles alley, which had been at the Duke's Head for very many years, was moved in 1990 to the Duke of Devonshire, in Balham (Page 8).

The Duke's Head in 1920 (left) and the Half Moon during the Second World War.

Half Moon
93 Lower Richmond Road
London SW15
081-788 2387
Grand Victorian pub with two bars.
Live music in separate room.

The **Half Moon**, also first leased in 1832 by Young & Bainbridge from an original 1817 lease, was rebuilt first in 1833. The property book notes in 1857: "These premises were rebuilt by us at a heavy outlay. They are let at £70 per annum. They command a good business." Young & Co bought the freehold in 1899 and again rebuilt the Half Moon in 1903, this time taking in the cottages next door. The Half Moon is now a well known folk, jazz and rock venue.

Redhill

Redhill was originally part of the parish of Reigate, but had always had its own market. In 1839, Robson's Commercial Directory remarks: "It contains 1,760 acres; assessed to the Property Tax in 1815 at only £1,096. The population in 1801 was returned at 112, and in 1831 at 221. It is south of Walton Heath and west of Gatton Park on the road to Reigate." By the end of the 19th century, however, the population had grown enough for Redhill to become separate from Reigate.

Home Cottage
Redstone Hill
Redhill
Surrey
0737-762771
Traditional old pub just off the A25.
Family eating area.
Conservatory.
Tables outside.

The first mention of the **Home Cottage** is in 1855, when it appears in Kelly's Directory of Surrey. The Starr family ran the pub for 91 years from 1887. Miss Sybil Starr, grand-daughter of the first Mrs Starr and herself licensee since the Second World War, sold the Home Cottage to Young & Co in 1978 because, she said, "their beer is best". In 1987, Sybil Starr attended a party to celebrate the centenary of her family's arrival at the Home Cottage. She died in 1989, only six weeks before her 90th birthday.

Left: the Home Cottage in 1937, when the Starr family celebrated 50 years in charge.
Right: Sybil Starr is toasted by the Mayor of Reigate and Banstead, Councillor John McFarlane, and Young's directors on the 100th anniversary of the family arriving at the pub.

Spread Eagle
141 Albert Street
London NW1
071-267 1410
Large corner pub between Regent's Park and Camden Town.
Tables outside.

Youngs carried out major renovations in 1979, extending the building at the back and merging the two front bars into one, but preserving the Victorian atmosphere. A row of five ancient beer engines, unused for many years, were restored to their former glory on the bar counter. The following year, the Home Cottage won the 1980 Top Pub competition organised by the Surrey Mirror. In 1990, a conservatory was added and a family restaurant introduced into the former stables.

Regent's Park

Regent's Park was remodelled from the old Marylebone Park, a tract of meadowland with three farms and cottages, by Nash between 1813 and 1827. It was then the furthest point north-west that London had expanded. By 1827, most of the villas and terraces were complete.

The **Spread Eagle**, between the park's Gloucester Gate and the bustle of Camden Town, is Victorian — a curiously shaped pub consisting of several houses knocked together. When it was built in 1858, its frontage was in Albert Street, then called Gloucester Street. It expanded to face Parkway in the 1930s, but only in 1963, when 57 Parkway was bought, was an entrance in Parkway added. Number 57 Parkway was originally 94 Park Street and was built in 1834: "the 27th house on the south side of Park Street reckoned East from Stanhope Street, the corner house inclusive", according to the first lease of the property. The street was then owned by Lord Southampton, built by William Clutchley, and number 94, a house with garden, was leased to Thos Lothian Esq. The freehold of the Spread Eagle was bought by Young & Co in 1929.

The development of the Spread Eagle.
Top left: the original pub in Albert Street,
1920. Top right: the expansion into Parkway,
still without an entrance in this 1940 picture.
Bottom left: the redesigned frontage in Albert
Street at the same time. Bottom right: the pub
in 1991, showing how the corner site has been
redeveloped to complete the building.

Richmond-upon-Thames

Richmond began life as a village called Shene (modified from Syenes, meaning shining and beautiful) and was changed to Richmond by Henry VII because he was the Earl of Richmond in Yorkshire. The name Sheen remained to the east but from then on, the area around the Old Palace was known as Richmond.

One of the oldest pubs in the town, the **Waterman's Arms** was originally called the King's Head "at the Ferry in Richmond" and dates back to at least 1660. In 1668, a token was struck bearing the inscription: "O.IOHN.RAN-DELL. 1668. The Watermans Arms. R.IN.RICHMOND. HIS HALFE PENNY. I.S.R." Water Lane was known as Town Lane from 1651 to 1712 and sometimes Thames Lane. It housed many of the watermen, either in tumbledown cottages or as lodgers in the inns. The Waterman's Arms was first leased by Young & Bainbridge in 1859 as a beer house and bought in 1897. The original pub was rebuilt in 1898, expanding into the shop next door. It still retains its Victorian two-bar layout.

Waterman's Arms
12 Water Lane
Richmond-upon-Thames
Surrey
081-940 2893
Small, two-bar pub in a narrow street leading to the river.
Tables outside.

The Waterman's Arms between the wars.

White Cross
Riverside
Richmond-upon-Thames
Surrey
081-940 6844
Grand riverside pub with a first-floor balcony.
Paved garden with its own bar.

The **White Cross**, first leased by Young & Bainbridge in 1869, stands on the site of the Convent of Observant Friars, built by Henry VII in 1499. A white cross was their insignia. The convent extended from Friars Lane to Water Lane, but the order was suppressed in 1534. On the evidence of a picture by Wyngarde painted in 1652 and showing the convent buildings, the White Cross stands on the site of the chapel where Catherine of Aragon asked to be buried. Her wish was denied by Henry VIII as the friars had openly condemned his marriage to Anne Boleyn. There may have been artistic licence on Wyngarde's part, however, as a 1649 Parliamentary Commissioners' survey refers to the site as a chandler's shop.

The White Cross is not definitely mentioned as a public house until 1780. Old prints show it was a timbered building in the early part of the 19th century. The present

A wartime painting of the White Cross and the riverside, now hanging in Young's brewery.

Old Ship
3 King Street
Richmond-upon-Thames
Surrey
081-940 3461
Old town-centre pub decorated with much nautical paraphernalia.

Orange Tree
45 Kew Road
Richmond-upon-Thames
Surrey
081-940 0944
Majestic pub near Richmond station.
Restaurant.
Tables outside.
Fringe theatre upstairs.

building dates from 1835 and is Grade III listed. It is possibly unique in having a fireplace situated under a window in one of the bars.

The **Old Ship** is known to date from at least 1735, when the Court scrolls carry an entry for it. King Street was previously known as Furbelow Street. A stage coach stopped six times a day for mail deliveries and collections en route to and from Hampton Court. The pub was first leased by Young & Bainbridge in 1869 and bought in 1897. It is possibly called the Old Ship to distinguish it from another Ship Inn in the same street. Today, it has a large collection of nautical equipment, including an engine room telegraph built into the bannister of a staircase.

The **Orange Tree** dates from at least 1780 and is said to be named after the first orange tree to be brought to Britain and planted in Kew Gardens, although it is a common name for 18th and 19th-century pubs. It was first leased by Young & Bainbridge in 1835 and bought in 1897. It was rebuilt around this time in the distinctive brick and terracotta Flemish style popular with the late Victorians.

It has achieved fame recently through being the home of the Orange Tree Theatre. This was born in 1971 as a lunchtime theatre in the pub's function room. The audience sat on old church pews. It quickly became well known for

The Old Ship (left) and the Orange Tree, both in the 1920s.

Red Cow
59 Sheen Road
Richmond-upon-Thames
Surrey
081-940 2511
*Traditional
old pub on a
corner.*
Meetings room.

its fringe productions, some of which were later transferred to the West End. It was the first licensed pub theatre of its kind. The theatre expanded in 1990 to an old school which had been fitted out for larger productions, with seating for 175. The pub won the Evening Standard Pub of the Year competition in 1976.

The **Red Cow** dates from the same period as the Orange Tree and was first recorded in 1809 as the Red Cow Tavern in "Marshgate". It was first leased by Young & Bainbridge in 1831 and the freehold bought in 1897. The Red Cow still has a Victorian over-screen, similar in some

*The Red Cow,
around 1920.*

*The Mitre (left) and
the Shaftesbury Arms
in the 1920s.*

Mitre
20 St Mary's Grove
Richmond-upon-Thames
Surrey
081-948 7318
*Cosy little local with prize-
winning hanging baskets
and window boxes.*
Tables outside.

ways to the snob screens at the Lamb in Bloomsbury (see Page 19). Victorian wood and glasswork is also well preserved at the Red Cow.

The other Youngs pubs in Richmond are all Victorian.

The land for the building of the **Mitre** was leased by Young & Bainbridge in 1853, and four years later, the property book recorded: "This property is not as yet developed. The buildings around are progressing very slowly and may never be finished. The value is quite speculative". It was, however, finally finished in 1861. It was leased until 1989, when the freehold was bought, from the Richmond Church Charities Trust, which may be a clue to the origin of the name. It is not known whether the windows, depicting a bishop's mitre and crook, are original or whether they are a later addition.

The Mitre has suffered more than its share of damage over the years. Two bombs were dropped on it in the Second World War, and during the storms of January 1990, the chimney stack fell through the roof, part of the parapet wall collapsed and the lower roofs were damaged. It was the worst affected of the 40 or so Young's pubs that were hit by the storms.

Shaftesbury Arms
123 Kew Road
Richmond-upon-Thames
Surrey
081-332 1372
Traditional two-bar local.
Prize-winning garden.

The **Shaftesbury Arms** was first leased by Young & Bainbridge in 1860, when an 1853 lease was assigned to them. It was bought in 1862. It was probably built in 1853 as some of the other buildings nearby display this date. It had previously been known as the Wheatsheaf and was originally a beer house. By 1878, it had acquired its present name and, like many pubs in London and Surrey, it was rebuilt in 1899 in a distinctive late-Victorian eclectic style. The main alteration since then has been the merging of the original two bars into one in 1988 and, more recently, the reconstruction of the garden.

Shakespeare
1 Shakespeare Terrace
Lower Richmond Road
Richmond-upon-Thames
Surrey
081-876 3301
Bustling locals' pub on the main road.
Garden.

The **Shakespeare**, on the way out of Richmond towards Mortlake, was also a beer house and was first leased by Young & Bainbridge in 1867. It appears to have gained a full licence between 1876 and 1884, when it was known as the Shakespeare Tavern and run by a Mr Henry Parrot. Development along the north side of the Lower Richmond Road, which was previously known as Mortlake Road, appears mainly to have taken place between the 1860s and 80s; the south side was developed later still. Shakespeare Terrace takes its name from the pub, which was there first, and both commemorate the belief that Shakespeare stayed in the area. The Shakespeare was rebuilt in 1900.

The Shakespeare in the 1920s, with a horse-drawn dray making a delivery.

Roehampton

Roehampton in Tudor days had only 14 houses, by the end of the 18th century 44, and by 1901 still only 285. The two Young's pubs in Roehampton belong to different stages of the village's history. The Angel is part of the old Roehampton, which was still only a hamlet, and the Maltese Cat is built on the 1960s Eastwood Estate.

Angel
11 High Street
London SW15
081-788 1997
Large, traditional old pub.
Garden.

The **Angel** is first recorded in a survey of the area carried out in 1617. Roehampton at this time had 33 houses and two inns. The Angel was first leased by Young & Bainbridge in 1872 and bought in 1880. Several small cottages

The Angel did a lively trade in its tea garden in the early part of the 20th century. This picture was taken around 1906.

surrounded the Angel in 1832, but they were gradually bought up and incorporated into the pub and its grounds. In 1861, the pub, then a wooden building, had stables, coach-houses, gardens and a bowling green. It was rebuilt in 1893 and altered again in 1935-36. The sign of the Angel is based on a painting by the 17th-century French artist Poussin, which is at present in the National Gallery.

The front of the Angel after the First World War.

The Maltese Cat in 1991 (left) and its 1961 sign showing the polo pony that gave it its name.

Maltese Cat
Aubyn Square
London SW15
081-876 7534
Modern building with two bars.
Garden.

The **Maltese Cat** was opened on 1 December 1961 and is named after the polo pony in Rudyard Kipling's story of the same name. The site of the pub is close to the old Roehampton polo ground.

Rotherhithe

Rotherhithe is Saxon for sailor's haven and most of the parish was originally marshland, the river frontage lying below the high water level. Docks have existed here since the beginning of the 16th century and the shipbuilders of Rotherhithe were the best in the trade in the 17th century. Many of the docks served the East India trade. Lysons, in his Environs of London (1792), notes that "the whole extent of the shore is inhabited by various artificers and tradesmen who make and furnish rigging and provisions for the navy" and by this time there were 11 docks. The captain and first mate of the Mayflower, the ship that took the Pilgrim Fathers to America, both came from Rotherhithe and the captain, Christopher Jones, is buried in the churchyard of St Mary's.

Ship
39-47 St Marychurch Street
London SE16
071-237 4103
Well restored old pub near the river.
Patio garden.

It is difficult to trace the history of the **Ship** accurately, as there have, not surprisingly, been many pubs with the sign of the Ship in the area. In 1825, there are four listed in the Licensed Victuallers' Records. The smallness of the streets near the church indicates their antiquity but the first definite mention of a Ship in Church Street is in 1822, when it was run by William Earl. As William Earl also had

a licence in Rotherhithe in 1801, it may be that he was at the Ship then. Unusually, it is one of the few pubs in England to have had two names at the same time. A sign on one side of the pub claimed it as the Great Eastern until it became a Young's house in 1985.

Shere

Shere, meaning bright, probably takes its name from the old name of the River Tillingbourne. It has been much used for making films and has been called one of the prettiest villages in Surrey. It is also the birth and death place of the county historian Walter Bray (1736-1832).

The **Prince of Wales** was one of three pubs owned by the Gomshall Brewery, based at the Black Horse in the neighbouring village of Gomshall and sold together with the brewery buildings in 1926. The Black Horse and the Prince of Wales went to Youngs; the third, the Half Moon at Ripley, is now a free house. The Black Horse was exchanged with Whitbread in

Prince of Wales
Shere Lane
Shere
Guildford
Surrey
0486-412313
Bustling pub with two bars.
Family room.
Garden.

The Prince of Wales sign, pictured in 1958.

The Chiddingfold Farmers' Hunt outside the Prince of Wales in 1960.

1990 for the Prince of Wales, Clapton, (see Page 37) and is no longer a pub. The Gomshall Brewery had been set up in the 18th century by a family of French Huguenots, the Reffells, and it continued in their family until the sale in 1926. The Prince of Wales is not listed as an ale or beer house in the Licensed Victuallers' Records for 1785-1827 and is therefore of later origins. Very close to the Prince of Wales in Shere is the place where Reffell's hops were laid out and prepared for the Gomshall Brewery.

The sale particulars in 1926 describe the Prince of Wales as having a tap room, a coffee room and a public bar; outside were kitchen gardens, lawns and a tea garden. Despite these amenities, the Prince of Wales remained a beer house until it gained a full licence in 1950. Within living memory, the Prince of Wales was divided into several small bars that were not connected on the inside and there was strict class division: the workingmen's bar had sawdust on the floor, and woe betide the farm labourer who by mistake entered by the wrong door!

Southwark

Both the Young's pubs in Southwark are modern replacements of 19th-century pubs that were demolished under council improvement schemes. They first became Young's houses in 1956 when the Founders' Arms was bought freehold and a lease taken on the Prince William Henry. Southwark had suffered bad bomb damage during the war and redevelopment of the Blackfriars Bridge and Bankside area was not unexpected.

The present **Founders' Arms** was built in 1979 and opened by the Dean of St Paul's in 1980. It has wonderful views over the Thames to St Paul's and is much nearer the river than the pub it replaced. The old Founders' Arms, probably built between 1807 and 1826, closed its doors in 1973 before being demolished to make way for Southwark Council's new development, Bankside Reach. It was at 56 Hopton Street, which for a time was called Holland Street, behind Founders Wharf, whence, presumably, the name of the pub comes.

The history of the streets in this area is confusing and names have changed several times. Before being Holland Street or Hopton Street, the road had been a branch of Green Walk. Hopton Street was named after Charles Hopton, who had bequeathed money for almshouses built in 1752. Bankside is, next to Borough High Street, probably

Founders' Arms
Bankside
52 Hopton Street
London SE1
071-928 1899
Traditional pub inside a modern building, facing St Paul's across the Thames.
Riverside terrace.
Restaurant.

Above: the old Founders' Arms, which closed in 1973. Below: the new building in 1980.

the oldest road in the area. This part of Southwark was notorious for brothels in the 16th century and Holland Street itself is said to have been the site of a notorious "stew" frequented by James II and his court. Bear-baiting and both the Rose and Globe theatres were nearby. Even earlier, Holland Street was the site of an ancient manor house and Bankside Power station now stands over the site of an old tide-mill.

The sign of the Founders' Arms is found only in 19th-century taverns. There is no evidence of an old foundry immediately on the site of Founders Wharf or the Founders' Arms, although there was an iron foundry in the late 18th century near Falcon Wharf, further to the east, and this may also be the origin of the name.

When the new pub was finished, it was ready to serve customers 11 months before it could officially open because the roads and paths through the new Bankside Reach hadn't been completed. The Worshipful Company of Founders presented the Founders' Arms with a bell cast at Whitechapel, the only foundry now left in London. Close by in Hopton Street is Bankside Gallery which is the headquarters of the Royal Watercolour Society and the Royal Society of Painters, Etchers and Engravers.

The **Prince William Henry** takes its name from the prince who became William IV in 1830. The third son of George III, he didn't come to the throne until he was 64 and reigned for only seven years before his death in 1837. Blackfriars Road was previously known as Great Surrey Street and may at some time have also been called St George's Road. Unfortunately, it is not known whether the

Prince William Henry
217 Blackfriars Road
London SE1
071-928 2474
Modern pub with traditional features.
Tables outside.

The old Prince William Henry in 1956 (left) and its modern replacement, pictured in 1991.

original Prince William Henry was built before 1830 while William was still a prince. In any case, it was replaced with a late-Victorian building in 1892 and this building, in turn, was demolished in 1974 to make way for new development. Like the Founders' Arms, it was not on the exact site of the new pub and there was also a gap between demolition and replacement, so Youngs went unrepresented in the area until the new Prince William Henry was opened in 1975.

Stepney

Stepney had been a village since Saxon times and the **Queen's Head** is built on land originally owned by Henry Colet, mercer and Lord Mayor of London in 1486 and 1495. He died in Stepney in 1505. The estate was surrendered to the Mercers' Company in 1518 and included the eastern side of the village street, with houses, dairy farms and market gardens. In 1810, the Commercial Road Turnpike was opened to link the docks with warehouses in the City and in 1817, the Mercers' Company began to grant building leases in the fields along the Commercial Road. By 1822, houses were being built around York Square and the Queen's Head soon followed in 1826. It was leased by Young & Bainbridge in 1831.

The Queen's Head was visited in July 1987 by the Queen Mother as part of a tour arranged by the London Gardens Society. She was invited behind the bar to pull a pint and when she was simultaneously offered a glass of Champagne, she replied: "Never mind the Champagne. This is much better." She promptly obliged a horde of Fleet

Queen's Head
8 Flamborough Street
London E14
071-790 6481
Typical East London local, thought to have been the model for the Queen Vic in EastEnders. The Queen Mother has drunk the beer here.

The Queen Mother arrives at the Queen's Head in 1987 (left) and goes on to pull herself a pint of Young's Special.

Street photographers by polishing off almost a pint of Young's Special. The event is recorded on a plaque inside the pub and in almost every Young's house through poster-size pictures approved by Clarence House.

Holland's, just off the Commercial Road, is another achetypal East End pub, bought by Youngs in September 1991. It had been owned and run for 150 years by the Holland family, who changed its name from the Exmouth Arms in the 1970s. It is Grade II listed for its original Victorian interior, including snob screens similar to those at the Lamb in Bloomsbury (see Page 19).

Holland's
7-9 Exmouth Street
Brayford Square
London E1
071-790 3057
Magnificently preserved East End local surrounded by modern development.
Piano.
Tables outside.

Holland's, just before Youngs took over in 1991.

Streatham

Streatham, like Tooting and Balham, owes its origins to Roman settlement around Stane Street. By the end of the 17th century, when spa waters had been discovered, Streatham was a scattered line of houses over a mile long, centred on St Leonard's Church.

The **Pied Bull** was one of several inns providing a stopping place for coaches along the road to London and has been in existence since at least 1768. From 1821, the stables and chaise (or carriage) house next door were acquired by the leaseholders of the pub, which suggests that the Pied Bull was small and had been without its own stables. It was first leased by Young & Bainbridge in 1832.

Streatham meanwhile was expanding rapidly. In 1841, the population was 6,000 — large for the time — but with the arrival of the railway in 1856, development took off.

Pied Bull
498 Streatham High Road
London SW16
081-764 4003
Splendid pub on the main road.
Seats outside.
Restaurant.

The Pied Bull in the 1920s (left) and in the 1940s.

The population reached 20,000 by 1871 and 70,000 by the end of the 19th century.

In 1920, Youngs bought the premises next door to expand the Pied Bull and the pub was renovated in the 1930s. During its most recent renovation, in 1989, a large skylight was uncovered over one of the bars.

The Pied Bull won the Evening Standard Pub of the Year competition in 1973.

Bedford Park
223 Streatham High Road
London SW16
081-769 2836
Splendidly renovated pub in the town centre.
Functions room.
Garden.

The **Bedford Park**, further north and on the opposite side of the High Road, is part of Victorian redevelopment of the older part of Streatham during the transformation from village to suburb. It is named after the Dukes of Bedford, the final holders of the manor of Streatham in the 19th century. It had once been a famous and popular pub but had become run down before Youngs bought it from Grand Metropolitan in 1990. Extensive refurbishment was carried out in 1990.

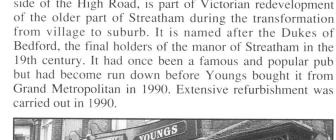

The Bedford Park on the day that Youngs took over in 1990.

Surbiton

Before the railway came to Surbiton in 1838, it was a small hamlet and the only house in the district on 18th-century maps was Berrylands Farm. Early in the 19th century, building started towards Kingston around the **Waggon and Horses**, which was built in 1812. Young & Bainbridge first leased the pub in 1831 and bought it in 1857. The Young &

Waggon and Horses
1 Surbiton Hill Road
Surbiton
Surrey
081-390 1712
Large, traditional pub with three rooms and public bar.
Garden.

The Waggon and Horses in the 1920s.

Bainbridge property book of the time notes: "These are rather old wooden premises but pleasantly situated by the roadside and with a good draw up for waggons".

Not surprisingly, the Waggon and Horses drew most of its trade from the carriers resting their horses before the climb up the hill. During the 19th century, an extra horse was kept at the pub to help any waggoner with the ascent and this horse's harness is still kept at the pub. The original yard — where George Cooper of Cooper Cars renovated his first vehicle — has now been incorporated into the pub.

Growth of Surbiton was rapid after Kingston had voted not to have the railway and Surbiton had voted for it. For a time, Surbiton was in danger of becoming New Kingston, but it held its own and its separate identity.

Black Lion
58 Brighton Road
Surbiton
Surrey
081-399 1666
Traditional corner pub with choice of bars.
Garden.

The **Black Lion** was first leased by Young & Bainbridge in 1840, when it was two separate houses. The New Age coach to Brighton stopped here. It was altered in 1854 and the 1857 Young & Bainbridge property book records: "These premises are held for a Term of years equal to Freehold at £10 per annum. The two Houses have been converted into one Public House at a very considerable outlay.

The Black Lion (left) and the Victoria, in the 1920s.

Victoria
28 Victoria Road
Surbiton
Surrey
081-399 3007
Full of ornate glass and woodwork.
Restaurant.
Garden.

The premises are let at £65 and carry on a very good business." The pub was bought by Young & Co in 1921. It was altered and refurbished in 1979.

The **Victoria** was built between 1840 and 1855 and bought by Young & Co in 1897. The nearest Young's pub to Surbiton railway station, and therefore part of the early growth of the town, it was extensively restored in the 1980s, keeping the fine Victorian wood and glasswork.

Sutton

Sutton is literally South Town and until the railway appeared in 1845, it was a village with extensive downs and commons grazed by sheep with "mutton noted for its small size and fine flavour". Even after the railway, Sutton took a long time to become a suburb of London, but as it was on the London-to-Brighton road, which had been laid in 1755, it became a stopping place for visitors. The Young's pubs

The Lord Nelson around 1920.

Lord Nelson
32 Lower Road
Sutton
Surrey
081-642 4120
Traditional locals' pub.
Garden.

New Town
7 Lind Road
Sutton
Surrey
081-642 0567
Large old pub on two levels.
Garden.

here are off the main track and products of a later age, however. The Lord Nelson and the New Town are in a part of Sutton known as the New Town, developed from about 1845 onwards in streets of small artisan-type cottages.

The first mention of the **Lord Nelson** is in Morgan's Directory of 1869. It was first leased in 1888 by Young & Co and the freehold bought in 1919. It has changed remarkably little over the years.

Lind Road, where the **New Town** is found, was the main road of Sutton New Town and is named after the singer Jenny Lind, who was at the height of her popularity in the 1840s. She is rumoured to have sung from a balcony near here. The New Town was probably built between 1869 and 1872. Interestingly, the licensee listed in the 1872 Morgan's Directory is the same as that for the Robin Hood

The New Town just after the First World War.

The Robin Hood between the wars.

in 1869, so the two pubs had a common link before they became Young's houses. The New Town was originally a Page & Overton house and was bought by Young & Co in 1920. It has also changed little externally since it was built, though the interior was totally redesigned and refurbished in 1977, when an adjoining house was incorporated.

The **Robin Hood** was built in 1867. A photograph taken in 1870 (More Views of Old Sutton — F. Burgess) shows ornate mock half-timber work on the front of the pub, which has either been removed or is hidden by paint and stucco work, though a small amount remains at the back. The photograph shows that behind the pub there were cottages, now demolished, decorated in a similar fashion. Young & Co bought the Robin Hood in 1899. The pub retains its pretty decorated windows, depicting birds on both sides of the building, and originally these covered three doors at the front as well. The pub was extensively altered and refurbished in 1985.

Robin Hood
52 West Street
Sutton
Surrey
081-643 7584
Friendly suburban pub.
Patio.
Functions room.

Sydenham
see Dulwich and Sydenham (Page 45)

The Abercorn Arms around 1920.

Teddington

Teddington, or Tyddington as it once was known, takes its name from the tidal reach of the Thames, which ends here. In 1861, it was still a village of 254 houses, but in 1863 a branch railway line finally arrived, a surge of development began, and by 1871, there were 1,034 houses. In view of the expansion in trade, Young & Co bought both the Queen Dowager and the Abercorn Arms in 1887.

Abercorn Arms
76 Church Road
Teddington
Middlesex
081-977 6720
Traditional street-corner local.
Garden.

The **Abercorn Arms** appears to have been bought from the Kingston Brewery Company and takes its name from the Earls of Hamilton and Abercorn, whose coat of arms it displays on its sign. It is probably mid-Victorian and the first recorded mention of it is in 1863. It was expanded into the shop next door in 1940, but it remained a beer house until it was granted a full licence in 1950.

The Queen Dowager between the wars.

Queen Dowager
49 North Lane
Teddington
Middlesex
081-943 3474
Ornate pub with two bars.
Garden.

The **Queen Dowager** was leased by Young & Bainbridge in 1860 and appears to date back to at least 1747. A small village beer house, it was previously called the Two Lawyers or the Jolly Lawyers. It was rebuilt in 1906-07 but, like the Abercorn Arms, remained a beer house until 1950.

Thornton Heath

Lord Napier
111 Beulah Road
Thornton Heath
Surrey
081-653 2286
Street-corner local, famous for trad jazz.

The **Lord Napier** stands in Beulah Road, which is named after Beulah Spa, founded nearby in 1831 over a natural spring famous for its magnesia-impregnated water. A park and a pump room were built but after a brief spate of popularity, the spa collapsed and the land was sold to builders. The Lord Napier was built in 1868 and first leased by Young & Co in 1884. In 1945, the premises next door were bought and amalgamated into the pub. The Lord Napier has been one of London's best known jazz venues since the late 1960s.

Parchmore Road is named after Parchmore or Passmore Farm, which stood here at the beginning of the 19th cen-

The Lord Napier in 1898, looking down Beulah Road.

Fountain Head
114 Parchmore Road
Thornton Heath
Surrey
081-653 4025
Large, comfortable pub.
Garden.

tury. It is probable that the **Fountain Head** is built over the farm and what was Leather Bottle Field. The name of the pub suggests that, like the Lord Napier, it has connections with Beulah Spa. By 1865, the farm had vanished and this is the date of the first mention of the pub. Cottages along the new Parchmore Road had also been built and there was a smithy next to the pub. Young & Co first took a lease of the Fountain Head in 1896. Just after the First World War, the pub was completely rebuilt when the road lay-out was changed and in 1922, Youngs bought it outright.

The Important and Valuable FREEHOLD

FULLY-LICENSED PREMISES

KNOWN AS

" The Fountain Head," Parchmore Rd.

TOGETHER WITH THE

Detached Shop and Dwelling House

KNOWN AS

112, PARCHMORE ROAD, with Workshop in rear

Right: details of the sale of the Fountain Head in 1922. Below: the pub at the time.

ES, Nos. 116 & 118, Sandfield Place,

was re-built a few years ago at a considerable cost, d Rough Cast Gabled Structure, with tiled roof, containing—

oms, Bath Room, Lavatory, Drawing Room, and Large

m, Office, Smoking Room, Kitchen and Scullery, Spacious blic, and Saloon Bars, with private Entrance at side, and raw-in in Front.

l Tiled Skittle Alley ; Detached Stabling, comprising Three ; Coach House ; and Small Stable at back and Lavatory t Bowling Green, Kitchen and Flower Gardens.

rises a Brick Built and Slated Detached Shop, with living a Yard and Brick and Tiled Workshop at Rear.

-are TWO COTTAGES, Brick Built and Tiled, with Gardens, 116 & 118, SANDFIELD PLACE

Railway Telegraph
19 Brigstock Road
Thornton Heath
Surrey
081-684 5809
Imposing town-centre pub
with a choice of bars.
Garden.

The name of the **Railway Telegraph** commemorates the first use of the electric telegraph in an event of national significance. People had been sceptical about the practical uses of this new service when it was introduced in 1837, but the first telegraph station was nevertheless built at Slough in 1844. It was not to gain public acceptance until the murder of a young woman at Slough. The murderer tried to escape by train to London but the police at Slough had quickly discovered the crime and decided to try out the new electric telegraph to send a message ahead to London.

The message arrived in time for the police to get to Paddington and observe the man getting down from the train. But because they did not consider the telegraph to be ample reason to arrest him, they decided to follow him for several days, by which time the appropriate warrant was obtained and he was later brought to trial, convicted and hanged. These original telegraph machines are now in the Imperial Science Museum. By 1888 the mileage of telegraph wires in Britain had grown to 246,000 and the number of instruments being used to 67,000.

The Railway Telegraph was leased by Young & Bainbridge in 1877 and was almost certainly built in 1876. Brigstock Road was originally called either New Road or Colliers Water Lane. The freehold of the pub was bought by Young & Co in 1901. In 1989, the Railway Telegraph underwent complete refurbishment and a beer garden was added.

The Railway Telegraph
after the First World War.

The Leather Bottle in the 1880s.

Tooting

Leather Bottle
538 Garratt Lane
London SW17
081-946 2309
Historic old inn; full of character.
Garden.

The **Leather Bottle** and Garratt Lane became famous in the 18th century because of mock elections held on Garratt Green, opposite the pub, for the Mayor of Garratt. The event, which took place after each general election from 1747 to 1796, seems to have originally started as a protest against land enclosures in the area. The local population set up a fund to help fight the landlords in court and their president was called the Mayor of Garratt.

What started as a genuine protest by a few degenerated into a farce in which thousands took part. A contemporary observer noted: "None but those who have seen a London mob on any great holiday can form a just idea of these elections. On some occasions 100,000 persons, half of them in carts, in hackney coaches and on horse and ass back, covered the various roads from London and choked up all the approaches to the place of election . . . at the last two elections, I was told that the road within a mile of Wandsworth was so blocked up by vehicles that none could move backwards nor forwards for many hours. As an event it was encouraged by the local publicans who made up the public purse and anticipated great sales of the day to compensate them handsomely."

The candidates were often the most bizarre looking to

heighten the sense of farce. One Mayor of Garratt, "Sir" Jeffrey Dunstan, was a second-hand wig dealer with a grotesque dwarfish appearance and a vulgar wit. He suffocated to death while being pushed in a wheelbarrow after consuming too much juniper. People were so fascinated by his appearance that after his burial, body snatchers made an unsuccessful attempt to dig him up again.

Valentine Green immortalised the scenes of the elections in some of his prints; one shows Lady Blase, wife of a candidate, passing through a traffic-choked Wandsworth with the Ram Inn and Spread Eagle in view; in another, outside the Leather Bottle, the candidate addresses the crowd surrounded by a guard of honour armed with brooms and mops. After 1796, the elections died away and an 1826 attempt to revive them was a failure.

Garratt was a hamlet of about 50 houses in the 18th century and 200 years earlier had been merely a house of the same name. Development along Garratt Lane itself did not gather pace until the late 19th century, much of it remaining estate and farmland until the 1890s.

The Leather Bottle itself cannot be traced earlier than 1745 but is probably rather older. It is listed as a building of special interest and in outward appearance has changed little over the past 150 years, although the interior has been altered. An old leather bottle of the sort used for storing water or beer still hangs in the bar.

Young & Bainbridge first leased the pub in 1832. The 1857 valuation entry in the Young & Bainbridge property book reads: "These premises have been occupied by the same family for a longer period than we have held them. The trade is remunerative. The premises consist of the Public House and a piece of ground adjoining on which are erected 9 small tenements." The freehold was bought in 1899.

Prince of Wales
646 Garratt Lane
London SW17
081-946 2628
Two-bar pub restored to its former glory.
Tables outside.

The **Prince of Wales**, a couple of hundred yards along Garratt Lane from the Leather Bottle, was built in 1852 as a house with stables. It was granted a licence in 1855 and first leased by Young & Bainbridge in 1865. It was well sited to serve the small, but growing community of Summerstown, a hamlet on the Wandle that contained mills and workshops.

The land the pub stands on — part of the extensive estate owned by the Spencer family in and around Wandsworth — was at one time called Garratt Little Green and the Surrey Iron Railway crossed it. When the railway

The Prince of Wales around 1920.

was closed in 1846, the land it had run across was sold off to adjoining landowners and the Prince of Wales was built directly over the old tracks. In 1898, Young & Co rebuilt the pub in the style it has today and bought it outright in 1922.

Castle
38 High Street
London SW17
081-672 7018
Large pub with several bars.

The **Castle** was first leased in 1832 and bought in 1899. Along with the Leather Bottle, it is one of the old Tooting pubs. Originally, it had steps down into the bar from the street. The lease of the Castle also included two acres of land in the Townfield, now Tooting Common.

The 1857 entry in the Young & Bainbridge property book reads: "These are pleasant Roadside Premises and do a large trade. They are let to a tenant who has been on the Premises for more than 50 years at the very inadequate Rent of £50 and are thought to be worth £100 a year. There is also included in this Lease about 2 acres of Land in the Townfield which piece of ground has been let for many years to the same party at £7 per annum and may be considered worth £135."

Two faces of the Castle.
Left, in 1920.
Right, during the Second World War.

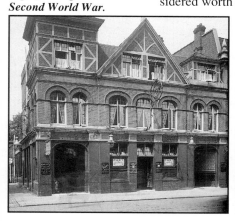

Gorringe Park
29 London Road
London SW17
081-648 4478
*Beautifully renovated
street-corner local.*
Garden.

The pub was rebuilt in 1901 in its present style, though it has undergone many changes internally over the years. In the 1950s and 60s, it had a music hall, featuring Peter Sellers, Danny Kaye, Boris Karloff and many more.

The **Gorringe Park** was first leased by Young & Co in 1892 and bought in 1898. It was probably built in the

*The Gorringe Park
between the wars.*

1870s. The pub gets its name from the Gorringe Park Estate, previously called Biggin Grove, one of several large estates that were broken up at the end of the 19th century for house building.

Twickenham

Like Teddington, urbanisation came relatively late to Twickenham, although it had long been a fashionable place to have a house. It was linked to Richmond with the completion of Richmond Bridge in 1777 and was well known for its strawberries and raspberries, which were sent to the London markets each day. Robson's Commercial Directory of 1839 remarks: "The greater portion of the ground from Knightsbridge to Twickenham is occupied by gardens and nurseries and presents extensive fields of unrivalled luxuriance, a large portion of the parish of Twickenham being equally luxurious meadow."

Old Anchor
71 Richmond Road
Twickenham
Middlesex
081-892 2181
A traditional old local.
Garden.

Building hit a peak at the end of the 19th century and in 1902, a tram service was established between Twickenham and Shepherds Bush. The **Old Anchor** dates from this period, having been bought by Young & Co in 1897 as a beer house, which it remained until granted a full licence in

The Old Anchor around 1920.

Pope's Grotto
Cross Deep
Twickenham
Middlesex
081-892 3050
Large and impressive post-war pub across the road from the river.
Dining area.
Garden. Tables outside.

1949. The pub was damaged by bombs during the Second World War, but not seriously. The building was altered in 1966, when the saloon bar was extended.

The **Pope's Grotto** takes its name from the poet Alexander Pope (1688-1744), who had a house on the banks of the Thames near the site of the pub, where he

Above: the Pope's Grotto before it was bombed in the Second World War and the temporary hut that replaced it until the new building (right) opened in 1959.

delighted in gardening and building his famous grotto. The gardens contained some of the earliest and finest cedar trees from Lebanon and a famous Spanish willow, cuttings from which were sent to the Empress of Russia in 1789.

The garden was cut in two by the road, Cross Deep, and the grotto was built as an underground passageway to connect the two. On either side was a chamber and these, with the passages, were lined with feldspar, marbles from Devon and Cornwall, and sea shells.

The best description is given in a letter from Pope to his friend Edward Blount on 2 June 1725: "When you shut the doors of this grotto, it becomes on the instant, from a luminous room, a camera-obscura, on the walls of which all objects of the river, hills, woods and boats are forming a moving picture in their visible radiations; and when you have a mind to light it up it affords a very different scene. It is furnished with shells, interspersed with pieces of looking glass in angular forms; and in the ceiling is a star of the same material, at which, when a lamp (of an orbicular figure of thin alabaster) is hung in the middle, a thousand pointed rays glitter, and are reflected over the place".

When Pope died, the house, gardens and grotto were sold and the grotto vandalised by souvenir hunters. In 1807, the house was sold to Baroness Howe, who demolished it and destroyed the grounds. She built a new house 100 yards to the north of the original. Later, a third house was constructed, also called Pope's Villa. The pub was built by Young & Bainbridge in 1852 on part of Pope's old garden but it was destroyed by bombs in the Second World War and the present building was opened in 1959.

Walton-on-Thames

Swan
50 Manor Road
Walton-on-Thames
Surrey
0932-225964
*Delightful old riverside
inn with many rooms.*
Functions facilities.
Garden.

The **Swan** gets its name from the ancient ceremony of Swan Upping performed each July on the Thames. Its object is to count and divide the birds between the Crown and the Companies of the Dyers and Vintners, each bird being taken up with a long pole and marked on its bill. The Uppers still stop at the Swan on their way to Staines in this yearly round-up.

The Swan was the place where, in 1910, the young Jerome Kern, the American songwriter, met Eva Leale, the daughter of the then licensee. Eva and Kern were married in Walton, Kern staying at the Swan, which was then a hotel. Kern was the writer of such famous songs as Ol Man River,

The Swan as it was when Jerome Kern stayed there in the early part of the 20th century.

Smoke Gets in Your Eyes, the hit musicals Showboat, Sally, Music in the Air, and the films Swing Time and Covergirl, plus a host of others. The story has it that Kern, while on a boating trip on the Thames with a friend, stopped at the Swan for a drink and fell in love with Eva at first sight as she helped her father behind the bar. Although very different sorts of people, the Kerns had a long and happy marriage until Kern's death in 1945.

The first written mention of the Swan occurs in 1770, when it appears on the Walter Leigh Manorial maps and was then just a small alehouse. The present building seems to date from the turn of the century. The Swan still has its own landing stage on the river bank.

The **Royal George** is named after a ship of 100 guns launched in 1788, which fought in the battles of St Vincent in 1790, the Glorious First of June, 1794, Isle de Groix, 1795, and the Dardanelles of 1807. It is now a modern pub

Royal George
130 Hersham Road
Walton-on-Thames
Surrey
0932-220910
Modern pub with traditional features.
Garden.

The original, Victorian Royal George (left) and its 1964 replacement.

but it was originally built around 1867 and bought by Young & Co in 1884. In 1887, adjoining land was bought, including cottages, but by 1960, the pub was felt to be too small and in need of extensive modernisation. The decision was taken to rebuild completely, taking in the land from the cottages. The old building fronted almost directly on to Hersham Road, but the new Royal George, which opened in 1964, is set back behind a car park.

Walton-on-the-Hill

Chequers
Chequers Lane
Walton-on-the-Hill
Surrey
0737-812364
Ancient pub with low beams and a modern extension.
Garden. Restaurant.

The **Chequers** was originally one of two village inns in Walton-on-the-Hill. In 1841, the population was 362 and the Chequers was being run by a Mr John Graham, brewer. It is not known exactly when it was built, although John Graham had a licence in 1815 in Walton-on-the-Hill, so we may assume this was at the Chequers. Originally, the inn included a brewhouse and bakehouse and there was a meadow behind. The Graham family stayed at the Chequers until 1903, when it was sold to I. T. Green, whose son, A. G. Green, sold it to Youngs in 1954.

The old outbuildings were demolished in 1955 and there were major alterations to the pub in 1956. The meadow behind the pub ran up to Breech Lane and in 1958 the top part was sold for building; the remainder is now the car park. The pub was extended in 1966 and 1973, and was altered again in 1983, with the addition of a new bar.

An undated photograph of the Chequers, probably around 1890.

The Duke's Head around 1920.

Wallington

Duke's Head
6 Manor Road
The Green
Wallington
Surrey
081-647 1595
Splendid old pub with choice of bars.
Lunchtime restaurant.

The **Duke's Head** is in the oldest part of Wallington, but until the railway arrived in 1847, it was no more than a hamlet and didn't even have its own church until 1867.

The Duke's Head was originally called Bowling Green House and is first mentioned in 1726. Between 1726 and 1773, it appears to have acted as a humble lodging house for travellers, becoming the Duke's Head some time between 1740 and 1806. At the beginning of the 19th century, the pub was a low thatched cottage of only two rooms, although it did have stables and a garden. The present building is mid-Victorian and was bought by Young & Bainbridge in 1857, although it had been supplied with Young's beers since 1832. A note in the 1857 property valuation reads: "This is a pleasant and commodious rural Public House doing a remunerative business. It is let at £70 per year."

In the 1920s and 30s, Youngs bought some of the surrounding cottages to expand the pub. During the Second World War, however, it was badly damaged by bombs but a notice on the old stable wall at the back of the pub still reads "Duke's Head Livery and Bait Stables". (Bait was a term for the feeding of horses.) It is a Grade II listed building and there are plans to convert it into an hotel.

The Ram Inn before the brewery fire of 1882 and (below) in 1920, before a later extension to the left obscured part of the brewery. The present Brewery Tap still carries the sign of the Ram Inn on the corner.

Wandsworth

Wandsworth was a large and thriving Surrey village before the Industrial Revolution brought a string of industry along the River Wandle. Industry had been here before, of course — the Ram Brewery itself dates back to 1675 or even earlier and there was also tanning, dyeing and flour-milling. Wandsworth became home to a large community of French Huguenots in the 18th century and they have left their mark both in the buildings and the street names. The history of Wandsworth is also tied to that of the Spencers, the family of the present Princess of Wales. Much of the land in Wandsworth was owned by Earl Spencer until the 19th century, and Young & Bainbridge both leased and bought land from the Spencers, including fields that are now part of the brewery.

It is hard to say which is the oldest of the Young's pubs in Wandsworth. The **Brewery Tap**, originally called the Ram, is presumably as old as the brewery and therefore

Brewery Tap
68 Wandsworth High Street
London SW18
081-870 2894
Large pub dominating the centre of Wandsworth next to the brewery.
Functions room.

dates from at least 1675. In 1690, the "Rame at Wansworth" appears in a list of taverns "in the Contrey 10 miles rond London". A hundred years later, Edwards writes in his Companion from London to Brighthelmston: "At the west side or angle formed by Garrott Lane, is a good established academy for young gentlemen, kept by Mr James Chapman. Opposite to which is the Ram Inn, kept by Mrs Acres. On the same side is a neat red brick house, in possession of Mr Tritton, porter brewer . . . Nearby a bridge over the river Wandle which is called the sink of the country."

At first, the yard at the back of the Ram was open and the pub did not look like a part of the brewery buildings but it has since been covered over. There was a disastrous fire at the brewery in 1882 and the Ram was badly damaged. It was rebuilt the following year, but was again badly damaged by the bombs of the Second World War. It was renamed the Brewery Tap in 1974.

The Crane, the Spread Eagle, the King's Arms, the Old Sergeant, the Queen Adelaide and the Two Brewers were all 18th-century pubs or taverns and may be even older. Those shown in the 1832 Pigot's Directory of Surrey are the Crane, the King's Arms, the Old Serjeant, the Ship, the Two Brewers (taverns) and the Spread Eagle and Ram (inns). The Crane is the only one that retains its 18th-century look and feel, however, with the possible exception of the Old Sergeant.

The **Spread Eagle** is first mentioned in 1780, although its origins are probably much older, and was bought by Young & Bainbridge in 1836. It was an important coaching inn in the centre of Wandsworth, where local magistrates'

Spread Eagle
71 Wandsworth High Street
London SW18
081-874 1326
Imposing pub with a choice of bars.

The Spread Eagle around 1920.

courts sat and other official and unofficial meetings were held, including the first meeting of the proprietors of the Surrey Iron Railway. The land agent for Lord Spencer used to meet tenants at the Spread Eagle to collect rents. The 1857 entry in the Young & Bainbridge property book reads: "These premises occupy a commanding position in the High Street with considerable frontage in Garratt Lane. They consist of a Tavern and Tea garden, a large Ballroom, a portion of which is now used as the County Court, a separate Tap which has a Licence of its own and a considerable range of stabling."

The Assembly Rooms in Garratt Lane, which were part of this large site, were used for concerts and music hall acts from 1860 to 1900 and the building later became one of the first Bioscope cinemas in London, known as the Court Cinema. It closed with the advent of the modern cinema and has recently been used by the brewery for storage.

The Spread Eagle was altered in 1874 before being rebuilt in 1898. Part of the land attached to the Spread Eagle was sold in 1858 and this became Wandsworth County Court, which was built in 1860. The bank on the corner of the High Street and Garratt Lane was also part of the property and was built some time after 1899. More was sold in 1912 to HM Commissioners of Work. Despite renovation and alterations in the 1980s, the Spread Eagle retains much of its late-Victorian wood and glasswork.

The **Crane** dates from at least 1748. It was first leased by Young & Bainbridge in 1832 and the freehold was bought in 1899. In 1832, it had a skittle alley. The property book records in 1857: "These premises are contiguous to another Public House of ours called The Bell but are well worth the Rent paid of £30 and perhaps more as a private House." The Bell, which was almost next door to the Crane, was demolished in 1935 when Armoury Way was constructed. It is not known whether the Crane is named after the bird or the old-fashioned lifting device the sign depicts. This part of the River Wandle was at one time busy with industry, and the Causeway was lined with small workshops and factories using cranes. The Crane was

Crane
14 Armoury Way
London SW18
081-874 2548
*Well preserved old pub
with two bars.*
Restaurant.
Patio garden.

The Crane, around 1920.

The King's Arms (left) and the Old Sergeant, both between the wars.

King's Arms
96 Wandsworth High Street
London SW18
081-874 1428
Large corner pub with contrasting bars.
Prize-winning garden.

Old Sergeant
104 Garratt Lane
London SW18
081-874 4099
Traditional old local with two bars.

Ship
41 Jew's Row
London SW18
081-870 9667
Vibrant old pub near Wandsworth bridge.
Large riverside terrace with barbecue.

partially rebuilt in the 1920s and the bar lay-out dates from then. The Crane, with its two small bars, keeps the feel of a country pub, although originally it had three bars. The third was the jug bar for off-licence sales. The pub is said to be haunted by the ghost of a small boy dressed in knickerbockers.

The **King's Arms** is listed as being used for Masonic meetings from 1757 until 1830. It was first bought by Young & Bainbridge in 1836 from Earl Spencer and was therefore, like the Spread Eagle, one of the first Young's houses to be bought outright. The 1857 entry in the Young & Bainbridge property book records: "These premises consist of a Public house well placed at a corner [and] a ground rent of £4 on which a good shop has been erected." The King's Arms was expanded into the shop next door and remodelled in the 1930s. The large and odd-shaped garden at the back, which runs down to the Wandle behind the shops fronting the High Street, perhaps suggests that at one time all of the land from the King's Arms to the Wandle was attached to the pub.

The **Old Sergeant** is recorded in Edwards's Companion from London to Brighthelmston (1789) as "the Old Serjeant, a small public house by Nash". The Licensed Victuallers' Records show that John Nash had a licence here in 1785. The pub came into the family via Henry Young in 1836, and was bought in 1857 from Earl Spencer. The property book records: "These premises do a fair business and are let at £50". The frontage has changed very little over the years with the coach-house doors still intact.

The **Ship** dates from at least 1809, and was first leased in 1832. The lease (dated 1834) calls the area Bridge Field and shows a dock called Public Dock on the Thames here.

The Ship in the 1920s.

The freehold was bought by Young & Co in 1897. In 1857, the property book notes: "These premises have been rebuilt by us and stand partly upon some ground formerly cottages occupied which lay between the old Ship and the River and blocked up the view of the same."

These cottages lay over what is now used by the pub as a garden and eating area and were bought by Young & Bainbridge in 1848 for the purpose of knocking them down, extending the pub and opening up the view. There used to be other cottages next to the Ship on the west side, but these have also now been demolished. They were still standing in 1918, however, when land was sold to the gas works nearby. This 1918 conveyance also shows another public house called the Waterman's Arms on the west side of the Ship facing the Thames. Just to the east of the pub was the old tram depot, now a London Transport bus garage. The present tenant moors his Thames sailing barge, the Convoy, alongside the Ship. In 1988, a conservatory was added to the pub facing the river.

The **Two Brewers**, which dates from at least 1800, was first leased in 1831 from Magdalen College, Oxford, which has owned land in Wandsworth since the 16th century. The 1857 entry in the property book notes: "This House is substantially built

Two Brewers
147 East Hill
London SW18
081-874 4128
A good, honest local in an enormous building.
Functions room.

The Two Brewers after the First World War, when it was also known as Jones' Wine House.

The Queen Adelaide between the wars.

and is let for £60 a year. There is only 2¼ year term and the prospect of renewal is not great as the Surveyor of the Estate is also the Surveyor of a large London Brewery. The trade during the part year was 80 Butts of Porter." Nevertheless, Young & Bainbridge kept the Two Brewers and in 1900 it was rebuilt. It was remodelled again in 1937-38, incorporating two shops next door into the pub. The freehold was bought from the college in 1974.

Queen Adelaide
35 Putney Bridge Road
London SW18
081-874 1695
Large street-corner pub. Garden.

The **Queen Adelaide** started life as the Queen's Head and was in existence in 1786. It was probably renamed the Queen Adelaide in 1830, and was certainly called this by 1835. Queen Adelaide was the daughter of George Frederick Charles, Duke of Saxe-Meiningen and married the third son of George III in 1804. He became William IV on his succession to the throne in 1830. The pub was possibly rebuilt in 1838 when Young & Bainbridge first took a lease. Young & Co bought the pub in 1915. Part of the large garden at the Queen Adelaide was once a skittle alley.

Grapes
39 Fairfield Street
London SW18
081-874 8681
Lively little pub, full of character.

The **Grapes** dates from at least 1833. It was first leased by Young & Bainbridge in 1841 as a beer shop and a full licence obtained in 1849. At this time, Fairfield Street was

The Grapes just after the First World War.

called North Street, and Barchard Street, at the side of the pub, was Red Lion Street. The 1857 property book records: "These are convenient and well situated Premises. They are let at present at £60 per annum. When the proposed County Court shall have been erected immediately opposite as contemplated they will be worth £15 or £20 a year more. The trade is good." It was not to be, however, for the County Court House was built in Garratt Lane. In 1877, part of the Grapes was a smithy and next door in Barchard Street a bakehouse. The pub was bought by Young & Co in 1899.

The **Alma** was built in 1866 and Young & Bainbridge took a lease in 1872, buying the freehold in 1883, when it was altered and possibly the painted mirrors that remain today were installed. The name commemorates the Crimean battle of the Alma in 1854, and Alma Road and Alma Cottages (now demolished) were built nearby at the same time. In 1987, the Alma was renovated; a decorative plaster frieze that had been covered up in what is now the restaurant area, was completely restored and other original

Alma
499 Old York Road
London SW18
081-870 2537
Beautifully preserved Victorian pub with rare painted glasswork and a French flavour.
Restaurant.

The Alma in the 1920s and its preserved interior in 1991.

County Arms
345 Trinity Road
London SW18
081-874 8532
Large pub facing the common; near Wandsworth prison.
Functions room.
Tables outside.

features, such as the staircase, woodwork, mosaics and painted mirrors, were all restored. The Alma is unusual in combining a traditional Victorian public house with the style and feel of a French bar.

The land for the **County Arms** was bought in 1850 and the pub built by Young & Bainbridge in 1852 on a piece of the Common known as Fair Ground, perhaps the site of an annual fair. Wandsworth Prison, formerly the Surrey House of Correction, had recently been completed and had been

Particulars of the sale of the County Arms in November 1898.

THIS DESIRABLE

SUBURBAN PROPERTY

WELL KNOWN AS

"THE COUNTY ARMS,"

Is remarkably well placed in the

TRINITY ROAD, WANDSWORTH COMMON

A thoroughfare of great traffic of all descriptions, on the direct 'Bus route from Balham to Clapham Junction, offering a fine opportunity for purchasing a sound Suburban Property.

---

*The **PREMISES** comprise :—*

ON THE UPPER FLOORS.

SIX BED ROOMS, SITTING ROOM,

CLUB ROOM, &c.

ON THE GROUND FLOOR.

SERVING BAR, BAR PARLOUR

SPIRIT ROOM, KITCHEN, SCULLERY, &c.

IN THE REAR.

CAPITAL STABLING, GARDEN, &c.

IN THE BASEMENT.

CELLARAGE.

Held on Lease for a term of **Fourteen Years** from the 24th June, 1898, at the Rent of £500 per annum, reducible while dealing with Young & Co.'s Brewery, Limited, for all Malt Liquors, to **£140 per annum.** The Lessee has also to pay as a further rent, the amount of the premium paid by the Lessors for insuring the Premises.

Part of the Premises is occupied by Mr. W. E. Buchanan, at a rental of £20 per annum, and the Stabling is let to Mr. A. A. Bastian, at £30 per annum.

The Premises may be viewed by permission of the Vendor, and the Lease may be inspected at the Offices of the Vendor's Solicitors.

The County Arms in the 1920s.

Wheatsheaf
30 Putney Bridge Road
London SW18
081-874 5753
Young's smallest pub.

Gardeners' Arms
268 Merton Road
London SW18
081-874 7624
Refurbished and extended local.
Tables outside.

The Gardeners' Arms before and after it was rebuilt in 1931.

open for male prisoners since 1851 and for women since 1852. In 1857, the property book records: "These premises are freehold. They consist of a Public House let at £8 per annum and of a piece of ground in the rear let for 70 years from Lady Day 1857 with covenant to build 14 Small Houses at a present rent of £20." The pub seems to have been small if it was let at only £8 per annum, the surrounding land commanding a higher rent. In 1890, the pub was rebuilt in the present, much larger style.

The **Wheatsheaf**, not surprisingly due to its small size, started life as a beer shop. It was first leased by Young & Bainbridge in 1867 when wheat was still being grown on the land known as Northfields nearby. At this time, Putney Bridge Road was called Love Lane and had been so called since 1548. Young & Co bought the Wheatsheaf in 1916. It has never been expanded and has remained a small, one-bar house.

The Wheatsheaf, around 1920.

The **Gardeners' Arms** was first leased in 1875 and

The Champion Stores, demolished in 1967, and the Pig and Whistle, which was originally to have taken its name.

Pig and Whistle
481 Merton Road
London SW18
081-874 1061
Comfortable and traditional local.
Tables outside.

Halfway House
521 Garratt Lane
London SW18
081-946 2788
New but firmly traditional pub next to Earlsfield station.
Small garden.
Family conservatory.

bought in 1915. The present building dates from 1931. In 1989, the pub was extensively refurbished and extended into the shop next door, to provide a bigger saloon bar.

The **Pig and Whistle** was built in 1900. It is likely that it was first intended as a pub but it did not succeed in gaining a licence, due either to Church influence in the area or to the fact that it once formed part of the estate of Sarah Augusta, who had put restrictive covenants on the use of her land when the estate was broken up in 1898. The pub then operated as two shops, 479 and 481 Merton Road, one of which became an off-licence, and both were bought by Young & Co in 1969. Youngs continued to operate 481 Merton Road as an off-licence until a full licence was granted in 1974 and the shops were converted into a pub.

It had originally been intended to call it the Champion, after the Champion Stores, a Young's pub in Wandsworth that had been closed in 1967, but the company decided instead to revive a traditional old pub name with the Pig and Whistle. The brewery chairman, John Young, arrived at the opening ceremony playing a tin whistle and carrying a piglet on top of a horse-drawn dray.

The **Halfway House**, opened by Young & Co in 1991, carries the name of another pub that stood at 433 Garratt Lane until it was demolished in 1976 as part of a council housing development. It stands on the corner of Magdalen Road on land once belonging to Magdalen College, Oxford. An earlier building on this site was a shop set back from the road. The fledgling pub was divided into two shops and one half of the present building had been operating as an off-licence since at least 1928. Young & Co acquired both

The old Halfway House, demolished in 1976, and the new version along the road, pictured on the day it opened in 1991.

off-licence and shop next door in 1986, the off-licence from Paines, the family that had also owned what is now the Clock House at Peckham Rye (see Page 81). Young & Co were granted a full licence in 1990 and work started immediately to convert the two shops into a pub, which opened to the public in March 1991.

Westminster

Petty France, now mainly famous for the Passport Office, became known as Petit France after the large numbers of French immigrants it housed. It had been called York Street for most of the 19th century.

Buckingham Arms
62 Petty France
London SW1
071-222 3386
Grand Victorian pub with one long, winding bar.

The Buckingham Arms, in the 1950s, when it was called simply the Buckingham.

The **Buckingham Arms** takes its name from George Villiers, first Duke of Buckingham (1592-1628), a royal statesman during the times of James I and Charles I. The sign is based on a portrait by Reubens, now in an Italian gallery. The duke, one of the richest men in England, was notorious for his arrogant and insolent behaviour and was assassin-ated at the age of 36 by a discon-tented subaltern in Portsmouth. The Buckingham Arms was originally a shop. It seems to have become a pub in the 1840s and was known as the Black Horse until 1903. It was acquired by Youngs in 1930.

x

Wimbledon

Wimbledon can probably claim to be older than any of the surrounding villages. Excavations of Caesar's Camp on the Common show there was an Iron Age community here. From before the Norman Conquest until the 16th century, the land of Wimbledon was owned by the Archbishop of

The Crooked Billet in 1920.

Crooked Billet
15 Crooked Billet
London SW19
081-946 5898
Ancient pub with mock-Tudor interior.

Canterbury and his successors until Henry VIII persuaded Archbishop Cranmer to give up the title deeds and the living connected with the parish in exchange for other privileges.

By this time, the **Crooked Billet**, on the edge of the Common, was already in existence. It is first mentioned in 1509 as a brewery and inn. It was closely connected with the Cromwell family, as are many other places in Wimbledon and Putney. Walter Cromwell was a "smith, an armourer, a brewer and a hostelry keeper" and he retired to the Crooked Billet in 1513 and died here in 1516. Walter's son was Thomas Cromwell who rose from the humble beginnings of a village smith's shop to become Lord High Chamberlain of England and Henry VIII's right-hand man.

The original building has long gone and the present one is mainly a reconstruction. In 1776, the Crooked Billet is recorded as being sited near the junction with West Side, but some time after this, it was converted back into cottages and a new Crooked Billet built on the present site. Edwards, in his Companion from London to Brighthelmston (1789), says that on leaving Wimbledon Common, "on the right is the Crooked Billet, a small public house, many years in the possession of Mr F. Wray." It was never a grand inn or major stopping place but probably merely a beer house on a

Hand in Hand
6 Crooked Billet
London SW19
081-946 5720
*Much-extended and
improved old local.*
Small courtyard.
Family room.

small scale. The hamlet of Crooked Billet is also small in contrast to the scale of the rest of Wimbledon and particularly the large houses bordering the Common. The oldest group of cottages next to the pub are probably late 17th century. Youngs bought a leasehold of the Crooked Billet in 1888 and the freehold in 1928. The pub was extended into an adjoining cottage in 1969.

The **Hand in Hand** is also in Crooked Billet and began life as a bakehouse. It is built on the site of a house owned by Daniel Watney, a farmer whose grandson founded Watney's brewery. The first written mention of it is in a lease of 1831 as "formerly 4 tenements near the Old Crooked Billet", sold in 1835 by D. Watney, miller, to T. Watney, mealman. It had by then become two houses with a bakehouse and outhouse. In 1869, it was sold to W.G. Holland, general trader, and by 1877, had become the Hand in Hand, Mr Holland describing himself as "beerseller". The pub stayed in the Holland family for more than 100 years until Youngs bought it in 1974, when it was still a beer house. It was soon granted a full licence and subsequently much altered and enlarged internally, although the original tiny bar at the front of the pub was retained. In 1982, it won the Evening Standard Pub of the Year competition.

The Hand in Hand, 1991.

Top: the Dog and Fox from the west in the 1920s.
Centre: from a slightly different angle in the 1940s.
Bottom: a view from the east in the 1940s.

Dog and Fox
24 Wimbledon High Street
London SW19
081-946 6565
Enormous building with relatively small bar area.
Tables outside.
Banqueting/functions suite.
Bayee Village Chinese restaurant (081-947 3533).

The **Dog and Fox** is possibly the oldest inn in Wimbledon Village itself. It is mentioned in a 1617 survey as "The Sign of My Lords Arms an Inn by Wimbledon Pound". It had eight rooms, two butteries, two barns and a stable. The present building began as a farmhouse in the 18th century and the name Dog and Fox is from the same period, first being mentioned in 1758. The land around consisted of several hundred acres. Between 1797 and 1799, it became a public house, although the farm land was still being leased with the pub. There were extensive outbuildings, coach houses, barns and orchards.

In 1797, it was being used for meetings of the Volunteers, a predecessor of the Home Guard set up to repel any Napoleonic invasion, and the land behind the inn was used to drill the men. At the annual fair, booths and stalls stretched from the Dog and Fox to the Rose and Crown, with a theatre and menagerie, but local landowners were anxious about the tone of the neighbourhood and the fair was suppressed in 1840.

In 1816, the pub was assigned, minus the fields, to G. Tritton, of the family that owned the Ram Brewery, and then in 1834 to Young & Bainbridge. The 1857 property book records: "This house is brick and timber. It does a large business and is of many attractions to a better class of publican." In 1869, it was rebuilt and set back from the road when the High Street was widened, but it still included "yards, garden, coach houses, stable, granary sheds, bowling green and paddock".

The Rose and Crown after the First World War. The garage on the right later made way for a car park.

Rose and Crown
55 High Street
London SW19
081-947 4713
Splendid old pub with contrasting areas in a single bar.
Garden.
Family conservatory.

The **Rose and Crown** was in existence by 1659. A trade token in the Wimbledon Society Museum bears the words "T.E. Heburne; in Wimbledon [16]59" and has a rose on the back; the inn was at first called the Sign of the Rose. It was possibly established in the 1640s by Sir Richard Betenson, the owner of Eagle House, next door to the Rose and Crown, and was called the Rose because Crowns were out of favour during the Civil War. A 1763 lease of Eagle House describes the mansion as house and gardens, 15 acres of land and the Rose and Crown public house. The Crown had by then been added to the inn's name.

The Rose and Crown became a local focal point during the 18th and 19th centuries and had to be much expanded. Famous drinkers included Leigh Hunt and Swinburne. Leigh Hunt wrote of the Rose and Crown to his friend John Forster: "When I find myself in the little room with the window open and the garden before us and a glass of claret on the table, care seems to be excluded."

Swinburne took walks along Putney Heath and Wimbledon Common from his home in Putney Lane and was a regular at the Rose and Crown, as well as the Green Man, Putney Heath, but after sketches of him drinking in the Rose and Crown appeared in the Pall Mall Gazette, he took to entering the pub by a side door and sitting in a private room. The chair he used is still at the pub.

Young & Bainbridge first leased the pub in 1832 and bought the freehold in the 1860s. The Rose and Crown won the Evening Standard Pub of the Year competition in 1970.

Alexandra
33 Wimbledon Hill Road
London SW19
081-947 7691
Four contrasting bars in Wimbledon's shopping centre.
Piano in public bar.
Wine bar/restaurant.

The Alexandra, 1920.

The **Alexandra** is a Victorian pub built for an expanding Wimbledon in 1876 by Young & Bainbridge, who had leased the land speculatively for the past year. In 1876, they were granted a licence to build. The freehold was bought in 1923. Major alterations were carried out in 1925-27, and in the 1930s, it was expanded into the shop next door on Wimbledon Hill. A restaurant, which was added at the side of pub in St Mark's Place in 1986, was converted into a wine bar, called No 1 St Mark's Place, in 1990. It was Young's first wine bar.

The latest chapter:
the acquisition of H.H. Finch

In August 1991, Young & Co took over the business of H.H. Finch Limited, together with its subsidiaries. This purchase involved Finch's 22 pubs and six Bill Bentley's wine bars and restaurants, mostly in the City of London, Westminster, and Kensington and Chelsea.

Finch's traces its history back to 1865 when the company was founded by Henry Hobson Finch. It continued to be run by members of the same family until the takeover by Young & Co. Never brewers, H.H. Finch had been concerned with public house management and retailing of wines and spirits. The pubs themselves have interesting and varied histories.

Dirty Dick's
202 Bishopsgate
London EC2

Perhaps the most famous is **Dirty Dick's**, which has been a tavern since at least 1804. Although the name is unusual now, it was not uncommon at the beginning of the 19th century. In this case, it refers to a Nathaniel Bentley who once lived on the premises and whose refusal to wash or clean up earned him the nickname. An earlier pub, called the Old Jerusalem, had reputedly stood on the site. Finch's

Brewery chairman John Young in the driving seat of a horse-drawn dray outside Dirty Dick's shortly after the takeover of Finch's in 1991.

bought the freehold in 1948. The former cellar has a fine vaulted ceiling and is now a Bill Bentley's wine bar and restaurant.

Duke of Wellington
179 Portobello Road
London W11

The **Duke of Wellington**, in the heart of the famous Portobello Market, has been serving residents, stall-holders and now tourists since Victorian days. Many pubs in London were named the Duke of Wellington after the Napoleonic wars. The freehold was bought by Mr H.H. Finch in 1890.

The Duke of Wellington surrounded by the bustle of Portobello Market.

Hoop
83-85 Notting Hill Gate
London W11

The **Hoop** in Notting Hill Gate, which had recently been known simply as Finch's but has now reverted to its old name, was also bought by Mr Finch in 1890. In 1957, it was sold to the local authority for a development scheme. A new pub was built and sold back to Finch's at a peppercorn price.

King's Arms
190 Fulham Road
London SW10

The **King's Arms** in the Fulham Road is also often simply called Finch's and is a fine example of a West London Victorian pub. It was purchased by Mr Finch in 1897.

London Spa
70 Exmouth Market
London EC1

The **London Spa** was bought by H.H. Finch in 1882, but had been operated by Finch's since 1865 when the company was founded. It is therefore the pub with

The King's Arms, Fulham Road.

The London Spa in Exmouth Market.

the longest connection with the Finch name. It is a friendly local, popular with the street traders from the market here.

Elephant
119 Fenchurch Street
London EC3

The **Elephant** possibly dates from before the Great Fire of London in 1666. It was originally the Elephant and Castle. The pub was rebuilt shortly before the First World War and was one of a number of pubs chosen in Licensing World, March edition 1914, to represent the "new" style of Mock Antique. These pre-First World War "olde worlde" taverns set a trend that was popular throughout the 20s and 30s. The pub has since been rebuilt again, however, and is part of a modern development, leased from Langbourne House Estate. It became a Finch's house in 1974.

Master Gunner
37 Cathedral Place
London EC4

The **Master Gunner** is a modern pub built on bomb-damaged land near St Paul's and bought by Finch's in 1964. Cathedral Place and the surrounding area are scheduled to be demolished but Youngs are expected to get a site within the new development.

One Tun
58 Goodge Street
London W1

The **One Tun** was bought by H.H. Finch in 1876 and is now a lively local near the Middlesex Hospital.

Wargrave Arms
42 Brendon Street
London W1

The **Wargrave Arms** was bought by H.H. Finch in 1894. In the 1960s, the house next door was also bought and the pub enlarged.

The other pubs that have come to Youngs as a result of

The One Tun in Goodge Street.

The Wargrave Arms in Brendon Street.

City House
86 Bishopsgate
London EC2

Queens
49 Regent's Park Road
London NW1

Three Cups
Sandland Street
London WC1

City Retreat
Shoe Lane
London EC4

the purchase of Finch's include the **City House**, which stands on the site of the Magpie and Punchbowl, demolished in the early 1980s for office development, and the **Queens**, facing Primrose Hill, which was tenanted by H.H. Finch and has been sold to Youngs by Bass.

The **Three Cups**, between High Holborn and Theobalds Road, and the **City Retreat**, off Fleet Street, have both been acquired from Bass as a result of negotiations over Finch's tenancies. They were never Finch's pubs. On the other hand, some of the Finch's pubs that were owned by national brewers will not become part of the Young's estate.

One unusual arrangement concerns the Walrus and Carpenter in Monument Street, EC3, which will remain a Charrington house with Young & Co as tenants.

Bill Bentley's wine bar and restaurant group originally joined Finch's in 1972 and will continue to trade under the Bill Bentley management. The six outlets in the group are

Bill Bentley's
31 Beauchamp Place
London SW3

Bill Bentley's
Swedeland Court
Bishopsgate
London EC2

Bill Bentley's
5 The Minories
London EC3

Bill Bentley's
Botolph Lane
Eastcheap
London EC3

Bill Bentley's
18 Old Broad Street
London EC2

Willy's Wine Bar
107 Fenchurch Street
London EC3

Bibliography

Greater London: Walford (two volumes, 1894, 1895).
Old and New London: Thornbury and Walford
(six volumes, various editions, 1881-1902).
London City: W. Besant (1910).
Victoria County History of Middlesex.
Victoria County History of Surrey.
Victoria County History of Sussex.
The Survey of London: Greater London Council.
The Art and Architecture of London: A. Saunders (1987).
The Buildings of England — London: South: Cherry and
Pevsner (1983).
The Streets of London: S. Fairfield (1983).
Victorian Pubs: M. Girouard (1984).
London Signs: B. Lillywhite (1972).
London Coffee Houses: B. Lillywhite.
English Inn Signs: Larwood and Hotton (revised 1951).
Coaching Days and Coaching Ways: W. O. Tristram
(1893).
The Old Inns of London: L. T. Stanley (1957).
Place Names of Surrey: Gover, Mawber and Stenton
(1934).
London Villages and More London Villages: N. Shute
(1972).
A History of Barking: J. Frogley (1900, unpublished).
A History of Barking: J. E. Oxley.
The Parish of Beddington in the Year 1837: R. Michell
(1975).
Betchworth within Living Memory: M. Ryan (1988?,
published privately).
Chiswick: Draper (1923).
The History of Clerkenwell: W. J. Pinks (1881).
Croydon — Story of 100 years: J. B. Gent (1970).
The History of Effingham: M. M. O'Connor (1973).
The Story of Esher: I. D. Stevens (1966).
The Story of a Village, Eton Wick 1217-1977: J. Hunter
(1977).
Hampstead and Highgate, the Story of Two Hilltop
Villages: M. Cathcart Borer (1976).
Inland Waterways of Great Britain: L. A. Edwards (1985).
Nicholson's Guide to the Waterways (South edition).
All Change, Kingston, Surbiton and New Malden in the
19th Century: J. Sampson.
History of the Borough of Lewisham: L. Duncan (1908).
A History of Merton and Morden: E. M. Jowett (1951).
A Prospect of Richmond: J. Dunbar (revised 1979).
Inns, Taverns and Pubs of the London Borough of Sutton:
A. J. Crowe (1980?).
More Views of Old Sutton: F. Burgess.
Tooting Rambles: F. Staff (1985).
Inns and Taverns of Walton and Weybridge: A. G. Martin
(1974).
Historic Wimbledon: R. Milward (1989).

Sources

Deeds and leases of properties, 18th and 19th century, held
at the Ram Brewery.
Correspondence relating to property from 1860 to 1990
held at the Ram Brewery.
Property ledgers from 1831 held at the Ram Brewery.
John Rocque's Maps, 1721-45.
Surrey Licensed Victuallers' Records, 1785-1827.
Post Office Street Directories from 1844.
Pigot's Directory of Surrey, 1832.
Kelly's Directory of Surrey from 1855.
Survey of London — John Stowe (1598).
Environs of London — D. Lysons (1792).
A Companion from London to Brighthelmston
— J. Edwards (1789).
Fulham — Faulkner (1813).
Various newspaper cuttings.

Libraries, record offices and museums consulted

Surrey County Record Office
Kent County Record Office
Buckinghamshire County Record Office
The London Library
The Guildhall Library
Surrey Local Studies Centre, Guildford
Valance Museum and Library, Barking
Dartford Museum
Dorking Museum
Grange Museum, Harlesden
Sutton Library

Photographs

The majority of the photographs in INN AND AROUND
LONDON are by commercial photographers who have
worked on behalf of Young & Co over more than 70 years.

Photographic sources known to the publishers
include Bedford Lemere & Co, Ewington-Cooper Photo-
graphy, Terry Smith, Albert Foster, Fleet Fotos, Editorial
Press, Michael Austen, Bredastudios, James Russell &
Sons, London Features International, Panther Photography,
Phil Weedon, Martin Russell, Thomas A. Wilkie, Margot
Bourlet, P.J. Loobey and the Greater London Council.

Alphabetical index of pubs